#spreadstardust

If you have found this book my wish is that you read it, leave a review on Amazon and then give it to a friend or leave it somewhere public for someone else to find. Don't forget to share your images on Instagram, Facebook & Twitter with the hashtag #spreadstardust and tag @emjandrew

Where I've been and who I've been with:

(Leave your name and where you're from before you pass me on!)

Foreword

"Everyone who terrifies you is sixty-five percent water.

And everyone you love is made of stardust, and I know sometimes you cannot even breathe deeply, and the night sky is no home, and you have cried yourself to sleep enough times that you are down to your last two percent, but

nothing is infinite,

not even loss.

You are made of the sea and the stars, and one day you are going to find yourself again."

(F. Butler)

One

2012

November had arrived and with it the typical English cold had set itself everywhere. I was sat outside in the smoking area, the chill on my hands tortured yet soothed me, it seemed like the only freedom I was allowed. Freedom isn't a world that I would associate with The Abbey; you give that away with all your sharps and pills when you walk in the door. There's no privacy or sense of personal space, instead you're encouraged to open your mind, bare your soul just so that when you finally venture back into the real world you can leave your shit at the door and get on with your life.

That's the idea anyway.

As I sat there, aged 21, contemplating the past 24 hours since my admission, I found it hard not be overwhelmed by just how fucked up my life had become; I'd lost nearly everything, including my life and all for what? For some god-awful eating disorder that had its claws burrowed into me and refused to let go.

The burning sensations on my fingers told me that I had smoked down to the end again without realising. I whispered a quick expletive and glanced up at the door where one of the nurse's beady eyes were set on me behind the glass. That's another thing I cursed. I couldn't even have the solitude of a cigarette break to myself. I hastily got up and headed for the door, deciding against lighting another. It was only the end of my first day after all; I didn't want to step on any toes, not yet anyway. The door opened before I got there and out of it came an unexpected surprise; tall, dark haired, arms I immediately imagined myself wrapped in and such beautiful eyes. Slightly flustered I attempted my first smile in what felt like forever and managed a feeble "hi". He turned and smiled, his eyes taking me in. "What's your name" I said with slightly more flirty confidence that I meant to. "Marc" he said in a wonderful welsh accent and then gave me a questioning look. "I'm Emily, it's nice to meet you" I turned and quickly walked through the door where the nurse was waiting for me. As I walked down the corridor, I felt a surge of excitement that I couldn't understand, his smile seemed to have warmed my whole body and my heart was racing.

That feeling left me as soon as I stepped through the door to my room. The plain walls and furniture surrounded me. Weak and tired I sat on the edge of the bed. Inside it felt as though my soul was screaming at me; there was so much going on, so much that had happened, so much that I had been ignoring and hiding from. I was only 21 but I felt as if my whole world was crashing down around me and there was nothing left to fight for. I didn't know it then, but this was the beginning of the rest of my life.

Two

2012

The Abbey is a formidable Victorian building
situated by the motorway in the South West of
England. Its position on the hill causes it to gaze
over the city lights, tucking itself away in the trees,
surrounded by high brick walls - hiding the
patients within. As we drove up the lane towards
what would become my home for the next two
weeks, in the gloom of the evening I noticed the
burning amber of the trees around me. Their
branches strong against the winter winds and the
only hint of weakness upon them were the fragile
leaves flickering like fire embers. I'd always loved
Autumn, the way the world lights up with colour
and fire, the beautiful death before the winter
months. This year however I hadn't even noticed
the change, I'd become numbed to most things
around me and nothing seemed to interest or
excite me anymore. I felt like nothing mattered;
I'd failed at my dream of becoming an actress in
London, moved back in with my mother after 3
years of independence, forced myself into a job
that I hated and had the social life of a nun who
had taken a vow of secrecy. I was done. My body
had started to give in to the constant abuse I gave

it; I wouldn't allow myself to gain any weight and I would scrutinize every inch of fat so that I had reason to hate myself, my constant purging meant that my body was in limbo and didn't know what was going on and my potassium levels were so low I could drop dead at any point. None of this scared me though, not until I had my first attack.

I was working as a sales advisor in a high end concession at a department store. The job was slow and dull, the ancient customers equally so, and my hour and a half journey to work each morning didn't make the day any more pleasurable. Despite having a resemblance of a routine my eating disorder was still in control; I'd skip breakfast making the excuse that it was too early to eat, if I ate lunch I'd immediately be rid of it not caring where I threw up and dinner was usually avoided or purged. That was my life, obsessed and repulsed at the same time. I came back after my lunch break one day to another lecture off my boss, the shop floor was at risk of collapsing because, horror of all horrors, some of the clothes had been tagged wrong. I stood quietly listening to her explain once more how everything should look and how the company expects things to be tagged and the room suddenly became unbearably hot. Usually my body seemed to laze in a temperature below zero leaving my hands and feet freezing cold to the touch- a quality none of my past boyfriends had appreciated in bed. The heat now however was strange and unpleasant, my bosses voice blurred and dulled and I half-fell-half-hurled myself at her looking for support as my legs were giving up.

"I'm fine" I murmured as the room stopped spinning and I was slowly dragged into the cupboard space that is the office.

"Put your head in between your legs and just breathe" she demanded and left me to it while I complied, gasping for air.

Something was very wrong, I held my head in my hands willing myself to calm down but as I did so my hands started to ball into fists. I had no control of my body, my hair was becoming more and more entangled by my cramping fingers and try as I may I couldn't breathe or unclench my hands from my hair. "Call an ambulance" I called out with the little breath I possessed.

My legs had joined in with the agonising

cramping now and I could no longer sit on the chair, I fell onto the floor as the girls from the concessions around us flocked to the cupboard fussing over me, finding the bin so I could wretch freely, trying to take my jumper off my soaking body. It seemed like ages before the paramedic arrived and we spent the next half an hour concentrating on breathing properly and working to unclench my body. I was taken down through the shop in a very ancient wheelchair, sharing the lift on my way with an old lady who to my amusement bent down to me and whispered "breathe deary" in a voice that itself seemed to lack oxygen. An ambulance was waiting outside where they spent at least three attempts to do an ECG and confirm that I definitely hadn't had a heart attack. For the rest of the day I was forced to lie down, my stepmother waiting on me hand and foot and my father glancing every few minutes as though to check I was still alive. I was exhausted, embarrassed and frustrated, annoyed that my body had failed me so dramatically. That night when I attempted to sleep I realised that it was the first time in nearly a year I cared if I lived or died.

Over the next week I had two more attacks, one on my way to work which left me lying on the side of the road in a very expensive dress, contorted by the cramps and screaming for help until the ambulance came and the last just minutes before my weekly appointment at Browns eating disorders clinic. It was the location of this last one that determined my next move into hospital. As the paramedics went through their final checks after once again getting my breathing to return to normal, I realised that Grahams' grey eyes were upon me, he was the big dog of clinic, the man in charge and someone who I'd only met twice before, neither under good circumstances.

"This is getting a bit out of control now Emily, it's time we made a decision about where to go next, I think you need to go to hospital"

I stared down at the floor, I'd been refusing to start day treatment at the clinic for months. I'd been once before and I felt like it had just made me worse, hospital seemed a bit of a drastic leap forward. Hospital was for really sick people, this particular hospital as far as I knew was for anorexics, there was no way that I'd fit in there. I wasn't that bad. However in the same thought I knew that Grahams' suggestion was one with only one right answer, according to him if I carried on, I wouldn't last the year, he wouldn't let up until I agreed to become an inpatient. I excused myself to think and sat in my old faithful car, lighting up a Marlborough menthol while I dialled the number of my oldest sister. She always knew the right thing to do and to say and for the past few years had become my rock. Ella was 8 years older than me and slightly shorter, we're often compared as we look so alike and our voices on the phone are identical, which causes confusion among our family and mutual friends but brings us constant amusement. I'd always been slightly jealous of her toned petite body and drive for life. She seemed set; husband, two gorgeous children as well as being a personal trainer and nutritionist. She was and truly is an inspiration; a pint-sized auburn-haired angel. I puffed away listening to her words, allowing them to calm me down and encouraging me to take the chance for treatment while it was available. By the time I had finished speaking to her, my mother had arrived. I had made up my mind and a few hours later I found myself in the back of my stepdad's golf, bags packed, petrified, Bristol bound.

Three

As a child I kept diaries where I documented my life almost every day. During my parents' divorce my Dad encouraged me to write down my feelings so that he could read them without my emotional attachment to the words and try to come up with a logical reaction for me. Some might find it strange that I never really had an honest conversation with my father about my emotions when I was a child, however after years of frustration I've realised that that is just the kind of human being he is; some of us are powered by emotion, others powered by logic and reason. Neither way can be deemed the right way but both have their advantages.

What writing did help me do though was keep a 9 year log of my journey through adolescence; something that I thought was purely therapeutic at the time in fact became a useful tool at 21 when I had to identify how my eating disorder had developed and thrived. The pages were full of frequent and ever-changing crushes, documented days with friends, endless family arguments and things that I thought that would be good to remember if I ever contracted Alzheimer's.

But when I did eventually look back through them I realised just how depressing these diaries were. As a 12-year-old girl I was significantly affected by a group of boys that declared to me that I wasn't pretty enough, I didn't have any boobs, I was fat and that my ginger hair was something to be ashamed of. "Sticks and stones may break my bones but words can never hurt me" definitely didn't apply to me, I took what these bullies said as truth and started telling myself every single day that I was ugly, fat, worthless and carried that with me throughout my life. Each day I wrote how much I hated myself, something that is hard to read back now as I realise how much damage I inflicted on my life and my self-esteem.

At 15 I moved schools and gained the new start that I so craved to have, things got better. I had friends, boys were interested in me and I started finding that life could be fun. I was playing a new role in my life, I was no longer the butt of the joke like some donkey headed Shakespearian.

Then came the mistake of falling for someone who would never truly love me back. To me he was the pinnacle of boys, funny, attractive and popular. I should have learnt the first time, after I got beaten up by his girlfriend who I knew nothing about. I should have told him to get out of my life when I heard all the rumours that he was messing around with other girls...I should have punched him when he broke my heart over and over again. But the fool I was never stopped loving him no matter what he did to me or how he made me feel.

I came to the conclusion that I just wasn't good enough for him, I needed to be thinner, prettier, more sexual and more interesting, someone that he could love back. This is where the villain finally took its opportunity and stepped in; the eating disorder, disguised as the solution to all my problems. It had slowly been growing stronger in the background because I had been unknowingly feeding it through my negative self-talk and beliefs.

I spent the next three years convincing myself I was over him: entering into relationships that would never work out because my head was too fucked up, drinking, smoking, partying, doing anything but eating. Every time that I thought I was over him and could move on, he would reappear and remind me just how I felt about him. Like I was some puppet that he could pick up and play with whenever he liked, and to be honest, I let him.

By 18 however, unrequited love was no longer an issue in my head, the only thing that mattered was the eating disorder that had buried itself into my life and grown with me, entangling itself into the very essence of "me". I still maintained great friendships, managed good grades and a job at sixth form but was never free from the torment of self-loathing in my mind. To combat the discomfort in my own skin I controlled my feelings with food. I'd skip every single meal possible and instead down litres of diet coke, drinking about 4 litres a day, if I did eat and if I had any choice in the matter it would usually be a soup or a salad. I told myself that I was being healthy, that if I was able to get thinner I would feel better and be more confident. The quote "Nothing tastes as good as skinny feels" coined by Kate Moss used to whirl around in my head. My school days in Malvern were some of the best that I had ever had, I was the happiest I had ever been with good friends around me and my developing issues with food weren't a concern to me. I was blissfully unaware of the road I was paving or route that I was starting to take myself down.

I carried on writing down my adventures when I left school and travelled solo to Australia in the autumn of 2009. None of my family were comfortable with the thought of me traveling across the world on my own but I had been unsuccessful with my applications to Drama School and had found out that my Nanny had developed bone cancer. I needed to escape from my life for a few months so I spent my savings on a visa and a plane ticket and a month later I was headed to Brisbane. I stayed with my auntie for 3 months, working at a restaurant/bar called the Full Moon Hotel. I met an Australian boy who made me laugh and kept me safe and we entered into a brief relationship until I left to travel the East Coast. Australia was an eye opener for me; I realised that I was independent and liked to look after myself, I could meet strangers and we'd soon become friends, I could challenge myself and manage difficult situations (although not when it came to food) and above all I discovered I loved to laugh. I ate with kangaroos, slept under the stars, worked on a mango farm, got drunk a lot, kissed strangers, danced on beaches and road tripped with people I'd just met. 6 months later, in 2010, I headed home to England with no money left but taking with me some solid friendships, priceless memories and a newly inked foot to the horror of my mother.

Back home things had changed and life had moved on without me; my friends were all studying at university, I no longer had a group of people I could call on whenever I needed, but worst of all I came home to find my Nanny a changed woman.

She was an inspiration to me as I grew up. When times were tough with my parents she would always take me in under her wing and I'd spend days and days staying at my grandparents' house, making cakes with my Nan and playing with my cousins. Her heart was so full of love and kindness and to me she wasn't an old woman at all. Nan had such life in her that she was always vibrant and smiling, keeping herself busy constantly and looking after the multitude of family members as well as her husband.

When I returned it was as though someone had replaced the woman I used to know. Nanny was frail, scared and had lost her drive for life. It was horrible to witness and such a shock to the whole family. I decided to move back to Cheltenham and into the annex of my grandparents house with my middle sister Leila so that I could start a Performing Arts Foundation Degree at university and be close to Nanny. Life became a lot more serious from then on and I no longer would fantasize about falling in love with boys or write about trivial things like how many sit ups I could do in the pages of my diary. Instead I would write about the frailty of life and would continually question why it had to be Nanny and how could life be so cruel. I found my eating disorder a comforting constant that I could control and it would take me away from feeling the pain and sadness that threatened to overwhelm me. My behaviours got worse and I found it harder and harder to manage, I was constantly tired and started to lose interest in everything, I would force myself to the gym every morning even if we had 3 hours of dance timetabled in and I tried my best to hardly eat at all. Inside I felt nothing, as if I was just going through the motions. The actress in me had stepped in, I managed to put on a facade, I smiled, I laughed and I convinced everyone that I was okay, I think I even partly convinced myself. It was only on a few drunken nights out when i'd drink too much that the mask would slip and I'd accidentally let one of my friends into my secret sadness and reveal how lost I was.

We lost Nan in March 2011. She died
around 6pm and less than an hour later the whole
family had gathered around her in the hall as she
lay there silent and still. Since she died I can't say
that I have felt the same - she took a piece of me
when she left and in a way I'm glad because I'll
never forget the magnitude of love that one
person can give. I truly fell apart after that
though. By November I was diagnosed as
clinically depressed. My middle sister Leila
moving out in June meant that I had the whole
annex to myself and would no longer need to
appear to be eating properly. I would plan taking
my own life over and over again throughout the
night. I withdrew from my friends, I stopped
trying at uni and often fantasized about dying.
Depression is a horrible illness that one can never
truly understand until they experience it for
themselves. It cankers the whole of your soul and
you lose all enjoyment and hope in everything. It
is not simply a case of "oh I feel really sad today"
or constantly crying - in fact more often than not
the sufferer will feel nothing at all. They become
numbed to the world and all those around them

and, try as they may, there is no easy escape. By the time I entered into my second and final year of my foundation degree at University in 2012 I was very ill; I had lost weight once more but still wasn't satisfied, I would spend hundreds of pounds on food that I would binge and purge on. Antidepressants made me tired and lifeless and I would often spend days in bed. I avoided people and would hide when my family members came to see me. By March, a month before my 21st birthday I was so weak that I collapsed during rehearsals for our final year performance and a few weeks later I had left University and started day treatment at Browns Eating Disorders Center in Gloucestershire for the very first time.

These memories were kept for years as I grew up, the emotional and physical abuse that I inflicted on myself was documented through my diaries and I would often read back through my life, tormenting myself by reliving painful memories, feeling nostalgic about the life I had and opening old wounds. It wasn't until I was 21 that I realised the damage that I had done. In a very dramatic and symbolic way I lit a fire and burned every single sheet of paper in the books. As I sat there watching each memory burn into ash I felt a satisfying sense of relief; the emotional scars weren't destroyed yet but the fact that I was making the first step of letting go was empowering. I realised that no matter what my past, there was always the hope that one day I could be free from all the torment, anger and pain and just be able to concentrate on living. That is all anyone can ask for in my opinion. The chance to live. The opportunity to change - to truly live and be happy.

Four

2012

I didn't want to get out of the car. I'd been asleep
I think for most of the drive up, I couldn't really
remember, my head was always in a constant
daze it seemed. We sat in the car park and I tried
not to let the magnitude of what was about to
happen crush me. I was going to hospital. Once
in, I wasn't going to be allowed to leave, I wasn't
going to have control anymore.

Mum and Joe were waiting outside for me to
get out. It felt like the longest time before I was
able to step out into the brisk chill. The darkness
was really setting in now.

Maybe I could run?

It really was bloody cold.

Maybe I could convince them all this has been one massive lie and I'm actually fine?

No use, my blood results were coming back with my potassium levels getting lower and lower; medically, on a scale of 1-5 anything less than 3.5 then the patient was at serious risk of heart attacks, muscle failure and sudden death. My result was 2.

Joe took my bag and we walked up the steps into The Abbey. Steps were hard for me, walking in general was hard. My legs always felt so weak and I never had the energy to move myself around these days, a simple flight of stairs would result in me immediately wanting to lie down and sleep once at the top. Pathetic. I felt angry at my own weakness. We made it into the reception area and I was so confused; this place didn't look like a hospital at all; there were carpets, a grand oak staircase, a chandelier hung from the rooftop and it felt warm. Hospitals weren't like this? Behind a huge mahogany desk sat a receptionist, who was personally way too happy for my liking. I wanted to punch her in her smiling face. I didn't want to be here anymore. I wanted to leave right now. She showed us down to the eating disorders unit, which looked less like the five star hotel reception entrance we'd just walked through, and more clinical and foreboding. Still not as petrifying as I thought though. After being shown round with Mum and Joe briefly, I began the admissions process. They took me to my room, which to my amazement had a TV in - I'd never had one in my room before. As children we were encouraged to play and have imaginations and instead of numbing us with bright colours and repetitive alphabet songs we played schools, made up plays and sang songs. Admittedly most games with my sisters would end with me being tied to the stairs or tied up and shut in the airing cupboard but overall my imagination is huge, and my knack for getting out of knots is even more impressive!

They went through my suitcase and my bag, looking for any contraband items. Pills were taken and would be given out each morning and afternoon from the hatch near reception. Anything sharp was banned unless supervised, which meant my leg hair would only get worse unless I wanted someone to watch me shave. Anything with a wire or lead was also taken away so I said goodbye to the flicker of an idea to hang myself with my straighteners. All chewing gum was put into the nurses pockets as that was also banned. It was starting to feel more and more like prison and I felt anxiety rising in me with each passing second. Then came the medical check. I asked Mum and Joe to leave so I didn't have to pretend anymore. I knew it would be uncomfortable, I knew there would be a lot of questions and I didn't want anyone close to me to know my answers, not yet anyway.

The medical check was the worst; I was stripped down to my underwear, poked, prodded and measured. I'd sunk down to 43kg at this point, 6.7 stone still didn't feel like it was good enough, it still felt too heavy to me.

I'd never been bothered about weight until I was put into day treatment for the first time earlier on in the year. We'd be weighed every Monday and Thursday and I hated every minute of it. Not only that, we then had to talk about whether our weight had gone up or down and how we felt about that. There's a lot of that in all types of mental health treatment; the dreaded question of "and how do you feel about that?" used to echo around in my head for hours. I became obsessed with weight during that first stint at day treatment. I was obviously the biggest girl in the group as I was the only one who wasn't fully anorexic. I felt like I stuck out like a sore thumb and every time I saw the numbers go down when I stepped on the scale, I felt that little bit better. Like I'd achieved something, like I was finally on my way to being someone better.

Fuck that was cold.

I'd started letting my mind wander and was suddenly brought back with a start when they put the ECG monitor pad on me. I hated them, I felt like I was some kind of alien experiment, all wired up, a freak. Weight check, ECG, blood test and a lot of awkward questions later I was done. It was all so surreal. It still hadn't sunk in; it can't have done when my main concern was the fact that I hadn't shaved my legs…

After that I faced a 20 minute meeting with one of the nurses there. She asked me everything: when it started, how it started, what I did, how I did it, if I would eat, what I would eat, did I exercise, how my family life was. It seemed to go on forever, and as we trooped through every question it got darker and darker and all I wanted to do was go to sleep. They explained to me that my toilet would be locked constantly. I'd have to ask to use the toilet and when I did, someone would have to stand just outside the door, which I wasn't allowed to close or lock. I was only allowed to shower before breakfast, and again, I'd have to ask. I wasn't allowed to be unsupervised or be in my room unless it was in the morning before breakfast or after 10pm. Meds were given out and taking them was compulsory. There was an Eating Disorder Lounge that we had to sit in during the day and we were only allowed to leave it if we had a group session to attend, needed the toilet or we wanted to have a cigarette.

The nurse urged me to get up at this point and took me into an empty lounge which was just opposite the ED Lounge. Everyone was still at dinner and unfortunately, I had to eat now too. She brought me in a plate of chips, sausages and beans and told me that just this once I would be allowed to only eat as much as I could. Normally we wouldn't be allowed to leave even the smallest of bites, everything had to go. You were here to be fed up and, in my view, scared the living daylights out of. No part of me wanted to eat the plate of fatty food in front of me, it was bad, it wasn't necessary, it was unhealthy. I wanted to scream and throw it in her face. Instead, I sat there while she watched, as I forced the food into my mouth. Bite by bite tears fell down my face.

Food is normally labelled in extremes for someone who has an eating disorder; there are 'safe foods' and 'bad foods'. Mine started out with the usual; bad foods were takeaways, chips, sausages, burgers, crisps, chocolate, anything processed. It then began to spiral. I added in: bread, butter, avocado, pasta, rice, any kind of sauce or condiment, cheese, most meats, anything from a bakery, wraps. In the end all I would allow myself to eat comfortably was plain soup and salad. Everything else had started to scare me.

During my time in London, only a few months ago, I had got to a point where I could eat normally again - well, as normally as I could. I had worked so hard to get into Drama School and to be healthy enough to attend. I was living my dream of becoming an actress. Every day was the same; porridge, fruit, sweet potato with chicken, more fruit. I lost all control of that routine once I left, and that devastating blow had killed any resolve I had left to be healthy. Once I came back from London I was lost, nothing mattered, there was no future for me, without acting I was nothing, and I was no one. Why should I eat? It was wasted on me. I was very good at hiding everything however; I became a habitual liar promising I'd eaten when I hadn't, being sick if I couldn't get away with skipping a meal. There was no more of that now though. Here I was trapped, and I had no choice but to conform. This was my worst nightmare contained in one building.

Once I had managed to eat a third of the plate of food in front of me, I was taken into the ED lounge to meet the other patients. Inside there were a group of girls looking painfully thin, but worst of all, painfully sad. It felt like I'd stepped into God's waiting room, the only sound was a dull TV blur in the background. I glanced at the clock - 3 hours to go until I could escape to my room and be on my own.

Damn.

I sat down on one of the sofas, numb, uncomfortable and tired. After what seemed like forever, two of the women started to talk to me; their names were Gemma and Karen and what I learnt about them fascinated and frightened me at the same time.

Gemma was 21 like me, but the things she

had already done in her life made me feel so unaccomplished. At 15 she had toured the world modelling, living in some eastern country on her own. By 20 she had curated her own exhibition at the V&A and worked as a highly ranked member of an art gallery. She astounded me. How could someone so talented waste herself? She was beautiful, talented, and clever. All that and yet she had spent the last few years becoming more and more ill. This was her third time in The Abbey. The only advice she had for me, which echoed in my head, was "Do this once and never come back."

Karen was slightly different. She was 43 years old, a military wife and had 2 children in their teens. Karen had spent her whole adult life in and out of treatment. I soon found out her self-worth was non-existent, as with most people who don't value themselves, however she had the one of the kindest and most beautiful hearts beating feebly inside her chest. She was calm and contained; her only giveaway was the sadness in her eyes. I used to watch her at mealtimes, it was hard not to, her demeanour shattered when the plate was placed in front of her. She'd sit with her head in her hands, or hands grasping at the tablecloth, every single bite looked like torture as she chewed, her eyes tightly closed as if in physical pain. It was unnerving to watch and so upsetting. It was only when she was away from the table again that she could smile and try to laugh, but it would take a few hours for the torture to leave her face.

I didn't meet anyone else that night. Most of the others were quiet or battling with their inner selves, so I sat and chatted with Gemma and Karen for a few hours until I realised just how badly I wanted a cigarette. I was escorted with another girl to the smoking area; it was brisk and quiet outside. We stood there in silence. I hadn't really noticed her in the lounge before; she had been sleeping all evening. Now though, there was nothing I could do but notice her. She stood there, wrapped in a zebra print blanket, puffing away as one of the staff watched us from the comfort of the warm doorway. She didn't look at me, the only relationships she seemed to have was with her cigarettes and her blanket. She must have been about nineteen…nineteen but so broken. The blanket may have wrapped her and protected her from the cold, but I could still see how bone thin she was, her stomach had protruded outwards from the food she had eaten at dinner and she reminded me of one of those malnourished children that you see in Africa. I was almost used to this look, it often happens that when you regain weight. It begins around your midriff and only disperses equally around the rest of your body once you are maintaining a healthy weight. She was shockingly tiny but nothing I hadn't seen before - emaciated people had surrounded me for so long that I was numbed from the shock of seeing their tiny frames. Her arm was the only thing that left the warmth of the blanket, and as she went to take another drag I noticed the plethora of scars and bruises along with a gallery of newly torn cuts all over her arm and hands, she had them all over her forehead too: battle scars against her body. There was a darkness around this girl, a hatred that seemed to cloud her and cut her off from everyone else. She frightened me and I was slightly relieved when she took her last drag and went inside leaving me to my own thoughts.

These were interrupted however by the burning sensation and my first meeting with Marc. Once I got back to the lounge I was exhausted, but once we were allowed back into our rooms I lay there for what felt like hours mulling over what the hell had just happened in those last 24 hours…waiting to feel some kind of emotion. No feeling came though, only sleep.

Five

I'm about twelve or thirteen years old and I'm
stood in front of my mirror. I'm wearing makeup
for one of the first times ever, hoping that it was
going to make a difference.

I hadn't really been a girly girl in primary
school: I played football with the boys, didn't like
pink, loved to get messy and dirty and thought
that playing horses or skipping was lame. But in
year 7 and the start of secondary school, things
changed. Suddenly boys became a species I didn't
quite understand. I had moved to a local all-girls
school that I hated; it was bitchy and there was
such an importance placed on appearance, even
though the only time we saw the boys from the
opposing school was on the school bus or at
specially arranged discos. I was getting ready for
the latter, petrified. Apart from a few that I had
known from primary school, the only male species
I knew there were of the "popular" crowd fame
and I wouldn't exactly call them my biggest fans.

Something about me made me a target for them: They'd talk to me on MSN messenger asking about how much I weighed and stating that "muscle weighs more than fat" constantly insinuating that I was too big. To them I was ugly, fat, my glasses were a joke, my ginger hair seemed to insult them and the fact that I hadn't developed any breasts like my peers was laughable. We'd go to town together as unfortunately the only friends I had were their friends, this was a prime opportunity to pick on me - throwing food at me telling me to eat it or laughing at my appearance in general. Boys went from being my best friends to people I should fear and be ashamed of myself in front of. I was desperate for their approval tonight but staring into the mirror my reflection showed nothing but fear. I had borrowed a dress from my sister in the hope that I'd be able to at least blend in with everyone else. It clung in all the wrong places. But maybe my makeup could be enough? It wasn't. That night the boys decided to put a bet on; who could get with the ugliest girl. They flocked around me, goading me to kiss one of them, I refused, I'd never really kissed anyone before and their pressure made me more nervous than I had ever been. My refusal caused them to begin a tirade of the usual insults, now with the added "frigid" mark against me. I tried to laugh it all off as I would often try to do, but the second I had the chance, I ran to the safety of the girls toilets. The door closed behind me and all there was to do then was cry.

Looking in the mirror again at the smudged makeup and puffy eyes I realised just how repulsive I was. Maybe I deserved this from them; I was after all everything they said I was. I was ugly. I was fat. They were right. I stayed there for the rest of the night and didn't come out until I could go home.

From then on I tried and tried to change the way I looked: I'd straighten my hair, wore makeup, tried to fit in with what everyone else was wearing, I started to throw my lunch away thinking I could starve myself and be as thin as all my friends. My resolve wasn't strong enough there however, I was still suffering from the pain of my parents' divorce and I'd often turn to food as a comfort, ruining all the effort I had put in at school trying not to eat. I began to feel guilty whenever I ate something bad, which led me to eat more and feel guilty all the time. My relationship with food had started to crumble.

I never really escaped from the fear they

instilled into me, despite making other male friends in older years and being pursued by a few, I didn't ever believe their affection was genuine. I honestly thought they were taking pity on me. I didn't start trusting boys until I moved to Malvern at the beginning of Year 10. My life and my attitude began to change and I was forgetting those bullies that I allowed to make me feel so worthless. I made the mistake of going back though; shortly after moving counties I attended one of my old friend's parties not realising they would be there. That night they hardly recognised me, one of them even tried to chat me up to my horror and slight amusement. I was still ridiculously nervous being around them though and drank myself to the point where I passed out on the floor. The next time I woke up it was the early hours of the morning, my head hurt and one of the boys that had made my life hell was kissing me. I felt sick. I was confused. I tried to turn away and tell him to stop. I didn't know what was going on. It wasn't until his hands started wandering downwards that I realised how wrong it was. I felt frozen. He was doing things to me that I had never done before and I didn't want to do. All I could do in my drunken stupor was roll over, away from him and his unwanted advances. The next morning I was told never to tell anyone, after all, no one would believe me, "who would want to get with you". Needless to say I never went back to another party there. I kept the secret though; it wasn't until I was in my twenties that I finally had the courage to tell my family. Even then I felt ashamed.

Years later I got my own back. I was 19, the thinnest I had ever been. At this point I had acted confident for so long I almost believed it and I was far from the scared little girl I used to be. I had moved back to Cheltenham after traveling and was on a night out with my two best friends. We sat drinking some strangely named drink, laughing and scouting out for boys and spying on unfortunate VPLs. I gazed over at the bar and suddenly I saw him, the ringleader of it all and the one I hated the most. He had grown up too; he had obviously spent most of his time at the gym since I last saw him. His face had the same smug smile on and I could almost see the arrogance radiating from him. My blood boiled. Although I was happy with having an eating disorder, at this point in my life I still despised him for making me hate myself so much and grinding my self-esteem to the ground. My friends noticed the change in me and clocked him straight away. Michelle had been with me at school in Gloucester and knew exactly what had happened back then; Louise however met me in Malvern so needed a bit of filling in. I sat there, frozen. Part of me wanted to run, part of me wanted to punch him, I couldn't decide which one I wanted to do more. The girls encouraged me to go to the bar, stand next to him and see if he would recognise me. The alcohol in me agreed. I walked over with as much confidence as I could muster and stood right next to him, leaning over the bar in what I hoped was an attractive way. He glanced at me and then glanced again. My heart pounded in my chest but I refused to let my face show just how nervous I was.

"Hey gorgeous" he whispered in my ear,

"My name's Rich, what's yours?"

I looked at him straight in the face; there was no sign that he knew me at all. He looked me up and down and smiled, my mind was racing….do I punch him now? Maybe a slap was better? Or I could just kick him in the balls and really mess him up, see how he likes it?…No, I wasn't as cruel as him…

"My name is Emily" I said coolly

"I'm the girl you used to bully for three years, remember?"

His face dropped, his eyes widened, that shock on his face was all the satisfaction I needed, I turned and walked away smiling, wiggling my hips slightly as I returned to the shots and my friends waiting at the table. That'll teach him.

I rarely thought about them again after that. The night in the club was all I needed for closure; the fact that I was able to change how I looked for their unnecessary approval but he would never escape from being an arrogant, shallow prick was enough for me. My life was different now; I had friends, I had flings, I could no longer be made to feel two foot tall. They didn't have that power over me now. They may have won all the battles but I won the fucking war.

Six

2012

I was surrounded by cream walls, light, calming. I hadn't slept much. I never did. By this point I couldn't sleep for two hours without having a night sweat; I'd wake up at least five times each night, freezing cold, soaking wet, shaking. I hated them, I hated having to shower constantly, it made me feel disgusting and as far as the doctors knew there wasn't anything that could be causing them. It must have been about four in the morning. I wouldn't be allowed a shower for at least three more hours. Ridiculous. I got out of the cheap sheets and peeled off my pyjamas for the third time that night changing into fresh ones, put my slippers on and crept into the corridor outside my room. Cigarettes in hand I walked down to the desk where one of the night staff sat and I asked if I could go to the smoking area. "You're up early" was the only thing she said to me.

I'd been half expecting her to put up a fuss -

they must be used to nocturnal patients. Walking out into the chill, the hairs on my arms were alerted to the fact it was November, I was cold anyway after the night sweats but this was a new level of freezing my tits off. It was better than being stuck inside and between wet sheets though - anything was.

Breathing in the fumes of my Marlborough my mind wandered. How had it come to this? How had my life plunged so spectacularly in a matter of a few years? I had been pretty much on top of my illness, I plodded along, obsessed but still able to function at least. Things really changed when Nanny died though, that was when the depression crept in and caused everything to fall apart...

Nan died on a Saturday, around 6 on the 26th March. Grampy had asked my stepmother, Dinah, and my aunt to come round and help him get her up into bed because she'd been on the sofa in the day. It had been one of the few days she had managed to leave her bedroom. Dad and Dinah had come through to our side of the house that morning and said that she wasn't looking good – she had turned yellow and they didn't think she had much longer left - maybe a few days, possibly a week. Even though they told me this, I was too scared to go through to the other side of the house and say goodbye. I don't know if it was because I didn't want to see her that ill or if I was still in denial, but I didn't go. I thought maybe I'll go tomorrow and she may be a bit better. Not going to see her turned into one of my biggest regrets. Dinah and my aunt were helping Nan up to bed and on the way, she died. Just like that. Nothing 'happened' to her as such; there was no dramatic scene, no famous last words. She just let out a big sigh, a tear fell down her cheek, and she was gone.

I only found out when my Dad rang me. Hearing his voice as he told me I felt my world fall apart. After about twenty minutes of uncontrollable crying and having to tell my sister Leila that Nan had died, my dad arrived at the house and proceeded to ring Ella. I asked if I could go and see her, then blindly walked through the playroom and into the hallway. And there she was, just there on the floor, lying in the middle of the hall. She just looked asleep. I half expected her to snore through her half-parted lips. I thought maybe she could be asleep. But she was yellow, that wasn't right, her chest wasn't moving. I sat on the floor next to Gramp who was sat on the chair, staring at his best friend and the love of his life. He hadn't even acknowledged that I had walked in. His eyes were full of her.

I couldn't sit there without touching her. It didn't feel real. She was so still; it was if time had stopped. Slowly shuffling over to my nanny I lay down next to her, tears filling my eyes as I looked at her beautiful face. I stroked her hair, shortened by the chemo; she'd only just started to grow it back. Then I took a breath and placed my hand on her tiny arm. She didn't feel cold like everyone says dead people do but she wasn't warm, it wasn't a normal feeling. None of this felt normal, like some horrific out of body experience. I lay there looking at my amazing Nanny. The woman who had been the rock in my life for so long. The woman who wouldn't be there anymore to make everything better.

I suddenly remembered being 15; it was the first time I had ever got drunk. We'd done the usual - drinking trampy cider in the park until 2am and I had stayed over at my best friend's house. That night I'd smoked my first cigarette, laughed a lot, played strip poker and drank Zed Lepplin cider until I passed out. The next morning I was unbelievably hungover. I went home and tried to tell my mother it was bad pizza, but when it came to driving to Cheltenham to stay with my Nan, I couldn't hold it in anymore and I threw up out of the car window. Funnily enough I was rumbled...After a lot of telling off and a massive argument courtesy of my parents, I was finally able to go and feel sorry for myself in peace. I didn't stop being sick for 48 hours in total. But as I was staying at my Nans I was well looked after. She lay next to me that night, all night. As we lay next to each other there was such a thunderstorm outside that the room echoed with the noise. She stayed with me for the whole night. Making me sip Coca-Cola to try to stop me from retching, stroking my hair and singing me to sleep.

Tonight, our roles had swapped. I lay there next to her stroking her hair and watching her sleep so peacefully, although this time she would never wake up. We'd never have a night like that again. Slowly our huge family arrived. Most of us lived either next door or five minutes away and everyone took the opportunity to come and say a last goodbye. We all took our places in the hall wherever there was space, sitting on the stairs, on the floor. It felt like Christmas; each year nearly thirty of us would congregate at Lynworth House - the house that my Nanny had lived in for over 40 years: sitting in the hall swapping presents, laughing, catching up, Nanny would cook one of her famous roasts, with every vegetable under the sun, at least three types of meat, around ten different desserts and we'd all be together. We were a force to be reckoned with. It was the only time you could guarantee the whole clan would be there, Nanny being the matriarch of it all. Most of us had lived there at one time or another. We had all learnt to swim in the pool that they had built, played tennis at the bottom of the garden and would spend sunny days having barbecues - playing rounders together and laughing. And here we were. It really was like some twisted Christmas. Although now there was nothing to celebrate and all the happiness in the world had left with her.

She was wearing a powder blue nighty that said "Night, Night. Sleep tight". Her arms and hands bare as her rings and bracelets no longer fitted. Her skin seemed faded and translucent. She was too thin; she wasn't the healthy Nanny that I had known for twenty years of my life. She wasn't the same and yet in this moment it seemed that I loved her more. That image will forever stick with me.

For months after I dwelt on those hours; how

I should have said goodbye to her when I had the chance, how I should have sung to her one last time, how I should have heard her tell me she loved me, how I should have told her the same. It petrified me that I was never going to see her smile again. You never really value just how important someone is in your life until they leave you.

One of the last times I saw her she was with a family friend in her room, she rarely left it near the end. Nanny had noticed my weight loss when I came back from Australia, and most probably before. But now she thought I was better. She was proud of me. They were saying how good my skin looked and Nan said I was beautiful. She told her friend that I had been top of the year in Musical Theatre in the first semester and Nan said she always knew I would do well. It was a nice conversation to be the last one. Nan always believed in me and always supported my dreams of being an actress. I think she believed that I could do it. She dreamt alongside me, always talking about me playing Eponine in Les Miserables, one of our favourite musicals. She would see it, she'd be there for my debut performance and she'd support me every step of the way. Every time I thought about this I would cry because now she never will. During those days

I would tear myself up unnecessarily, I longed to take her pain away; each night wishing that I could take her place instead, reasoning that I wasn't as important and could never impact so many lives in such a positive way. I watched her starve in front of me as she lost her appetite from the cancer and the drugs and instead of it driving me to become healthier, my messed-up mind vowed to starve alongside her. If I felt her pain, then maybe I could take it away from her. I deserved that, not her.

When you are malnourished, whether at a healthy weight or not, your brain doesn't function properly. You don't think straight, and most reasoning goes out the window. That is my only excuse for thinking so wrongly during this point in my life; I can't make up for my actions or my thoughts. After my sister Leila moved out a few months later I spiralled into darkness, only able to concentrate on the hole in my heart that seemed inescapably painful. At night I'd sit on my balcony willing myself to find the strength to jump. Every morning when I woke up I'd recite to myself "I'm ready to die now" over and over again, like some fucked up prayer. It got to the point where I took as many pills as I could get my hands on, locked away in my own room. Locked away in my own thoughts and unable to escape. I don't know what saved me at that point. I don't know where the sudden urge to live came from, but I realised what I had just done and purged as many of them as I could from my body. I was left exhausted, unable to think anymore, that night was the first night I slept properly in what seemed like forever.

Burning. My thoughts and cigarette had come to an end. I was tired. Slowly I pulled myself up from the chair and proceeded to drag myself back to my room, past the desk and informing the nurse behind it that I hadn't done a runner as I went. My sheets had almost dried; I had about two hours until I could shower, two hours until I would be faced with my first full day in The Abbey. I didn't have the energy to worry anymore. What would happen would happen. My head hit the pillow, my last thoughts drifted back to my Nanny again and I slept.

Seven

I'm lying on cheap sheets and sucking on a very contraband but very good fruit sweet courtesy of Fox's. Thank god our rooms had televisions; tonight's viewing, X-Factor. I was attempting to blank out of my mind the day's events…no use. The day consisted of bran flakes with proper milk, half a portion of chicken and rice that burned my face off as I was crap at eating anything remotely spicy, a peanut butter sandwich that made my mouth stick together and a vanilla Fortisip. The last was the part that angered me the most. Fortisips are building up drinks – high energy, high calorie, high fat, and high everything. I hated them. In my eyes I was heavy enough, I had enough fat and I certainly didn't need more of anything on my body. I needed less. The idea of eating three meals and keeping each one down felt like the hardest thing in the world, the added kick in the face of a build-up drink was cruel. I could feel the fat on my body taunting me. I wanted to rip it all off.

Ouch. I'd unknowingly clawed at myself again.

Looking down at my stomach a trickle of shining blood dribbled down onto the bed. My sister, Ella had come to visit me during the day, Dad and Dinah shortly after. It had done well to break up the day but it was tiring pretending that I was ok and that I was happy to be there on the outside, when inside I begged them to take me home. Other than the occasional visits all I seemed to be allowed to do was sit in the ED lounge, and all there was to do then was sleep. Now, I love sleep just as much as the next person, but 12 hours a day is a bit extreme. I was already fed up of having to ask permission to go anywhere. I hadn't been able to go to the loo all day because once I was sat on the seat and the nurse was stood outside, in my eye line, I got stage fright. My bladder hurt, my stomach hurt and my regurgitation was enough to make me cry. By this point my body was so used to throwing up anything that was put into it that it did it automatically, even when I didn't want to. Even if I ate something as small as an apple or drink some coffee I could spend the next 3 hours constantly being sick in my mouth and having to swallow it. I was so embarrassed and disgusted with myself I would do almost everything to avoid eating in front of anyone. The only way I could stop it was to throw up and get rid of it. If I didn't I would be constantly regurgitating until I ate another meal and it would all start again. A constant battle.

After the first day, every one after that was the same: pills, food I didn't like, regurgitation, food I didn't want to eat, pills, regurgitation, Fortisips I had to down like shots of Sambuca and the odd visit from my family. The only highlight to my day was seeing glimpses of Marc, I desperately wanted to talk to him, some unknown factor seemed to draw me to him. I wanted to know him, know why he was in there, know what had happened that could possibly have brought him to the same place that I was imprisoned. A few days in we bumped into each other in the smoking area and my wish came true. I had the chance to talk to this mysterious stranger and learn who he was. Marc was an addict and to my surprise his self-worth was as low as mine. During our chats I discovered that his biggest flaw was his own doing – his self-esteem was rock bottom. I again found myself questioning the world; how could someone so unbelievably breath-taking see nothing in the mirror. Not only was he blessed with good looks his personality was perfect; he was funny, kind, open, we'd laugh together and have proper conversations and for the first time in a long time I found myself opening up to someone and letting him know the real me.

One night after I was freed from the confines of the lounge, I snuck up to the corridor, past my room and into his. My heart was pounding. I wasn't sure if it was because he'd been topless as I entered giving me a view of his rippling abs, or the fact that I wasn't quite sure if I was allowed to be in there. Breaking the rules felt so fun. We started to watch a film but ended up ignoring it completely and just talking. I sat there chewing on some stolen chewing gum (also not allowed for ED patients) and discovered that he was addicted to cocaine and his habit hadn't been helped by his cheating ex-girlfriends. Something about him made me relax: I was so nervous and comfortable at the same time and my mind was constantly questioning why someone so amazing would be talking to me. As we sat on the bed, one of the Bourne films blurring the background, Marc asked me about my bulimia. He was the first person in the Abbey who wasn't staff to ask me about it and really seem to want to know. It felt strange and I was scared that if I did tell him just how fucked up and disgusting I was, he'd kick me out of his room himself. The boot never came. I found myself laughing again; he seemed the only person to make me feel comfortable in this damn hospital. I felt like a bird that had finally been let out of its cage.

Suddenly there was a knock at the door, we both jumped, it dawned on me that the first checks had probably been done by now and I wasn't in my room. Fun time was over. Shit. The door opened and in walked Jeff the night nurse, very unimpressed. I'm not sure what made things worse; that I was sat on the bed or that Marc still had no top on. I was ordered back to my room and left Marc to get a speaking to. Later on he explained that Jeff had politely pointed out that funnily enough The Abbey was not a dating agency and patient relationships were forbidden. I think we were both slightly embarrassed by this, after all we had both just thought we were getting on as friends….it wasn't anything more than that was it? Could it be? I started to wish that I hadn't read 50 Shades of Grey that month. I looked into Marc's eyes again wishing I could read his mind and know what he thought of me. It seemed Jeff had unknowingly planted that seed of possibility into my head and spurred my heart and head to begin playing a very dangerous game. This could get messy.

Eight

Every now and then I'd set myself goals. Something to work towards, but usually they'd never be completed. The only goals that I ever completed were recording my own album and becoming a size zero. Regulars were to stop smoking, become a size zero, find someone who loved me, tone up, get a six pack and skydive.

When I came back from Mountview - the drama school in London, I had been crushed. I had spent twenty one years of my life working towards that one dream of training to be an actress and after finally making it there in September 2012, things royally ballsed up in a way that they had never done before.

I lived in a house in Wood Green, North London. I didn't like the area one bit; it was rough and felt dangerous but that didn't matter so much to me because I was living my dream and finally on my way to becoming an actress. I lived

with two amazing guys; Doug and Simon. I'd
never had gay friends before but after the first
week I couldn't think of anything better. They
were perfect; we sat in bed and watched X-
Factor, I'd hear Simon sing nearly every minute
he was awake, Doug would play some of the most
beautiful piano I had ever heard and we laughed,
a lot and they were some of the kindest, most
caring souls I ever had the pleasure to meet. I was
eating, I was healthy, I was happy.

The one thing that ruined everything for me
were the night sweats. I slept on average an hour
a night, and during the day I was so tired I
couldn't even stay awake, not even during classes.
On one of the first days we had to do an
improvisation class. I sat in the group I was given
and we had to come up with a family scenario so
we were brainstorming ideas. In my head I was so
ready, so eager to get my Mountview dream going
but my eyes kept closing and my body stopped
responding to any of the external stimuli going on
around me. Before I knew it, I was asleep. I had
fallen asleep mid-way through a conversation and
what was probably a couple of seconds felt like a
few minutes. We performed and I remembered
nothing of it; my friends there told me I was hot
seated and came across as a cold bitch of a
stepmother who was so uncaring. Apparently, it

was convincing…I personally think it is just because I was too tired to look like I gave a damn.

It killed me. I was finally where I wanted to be and doing what I wanted to do with my life and I couldn't even sit still for a couple of minutes without drifting off. I'd sit in the cafeteria with my classmates, conversations washing over me, spooning couscous into my mouth trying to get some energy from the food. Nothing worked. I slowly dragged myself to the toilet, locked the door and stared down into the bowl; this was the part where I threw up. I didn't even want to. I hadn't been sick for nearly a week now but that wasn't even it; I had single handedly ruined my own life and now I knew what to do. With all the strength I had I turned and walked away from ruining my winning streak. I was NOT going to be sick at Drama School, I had promised myself that. I was so emotionally broken and so frustrated with my body giving up on me, when I was finally treating it right I ended up in the admissions office only a few days into my course crying uncontrollably on the floor, unable to even stand.

My gut was screaming that I couldn't do this, every fibre of my being felt broken, it was all too hard and I didn't know why I was incapable of sleeping at night. I was scared; everything I had worked towards since I was 3 when I took my first role fighting over who played Wendy during playtime in nursery, everything was crumbling in front of my eyes. The admissions officer managed to calm me down slightly; it felt like the hardest thing in the world to stop crying. She persuaded me to try a week and then decide what to do about leaving. I returned to my class and we had a sexual education lecture, god knows why, this was university after all…don't most people lose their virginity at 15 these days? Everyone seemed to be enjoying themselves but try as I may I yet again kept falling asleep, I couldn't laugh, and I couldn't join in as much as I prayed that I could.

Excusing myself, I returned back to the admissions office once more and told her that I had to go home. I wasn't able to be the actress I knew I could be, every minute was breaking me more. I wasn't good enough. Not now. I rang my mother from the office, the disappointment and frustration in her voice as she listened to me cry and tell her I needed to come home only broke me more. Somehow I got back to my house, I must have walked but I remembered nothing.

Back at the house I lay on my bed, tears pouring down my face and wishing with every strength I had left that I was dead. I reached over to my bag and found my antidepressants. I stared at the packets wondering how many it would take for my heart to stop beating. For it all to be over. There was nothing more for me now, I was nothing and I would never be anyone important or special, I didn't even have my talent anymore. While I lay there thinking about how best to kill myself, and do it properly this time without any chance of coming back, I fell asleep.

When I woke up I forgot about the pills and went into autopilot; I packed, I rang my father, I must have changed my clothes. My stepdad arrived later that night; we put everything into the car and drove back to The Forest of Dean. Away from everything I'd ever wanted.

On the way home I reverted back to a relapse prevention exercise that I had learnt in CBT; Problem Solving. You take the problem that you have and then list all the possible solutions available to you from sensible to ridiculous. If there was ever a time that I needed to use it, it was then and so the lists began. The only way to carry on living was to plan:

My Year Off _(If it's just a year)_

1. Work: 9-5 job, live with Mum until I can move out, find hobbies, see friends

2. Finish my degree? – if possible

3. Travel: start experiencing different opportunities, find different routes to go down

I listed my problems and the solutions available to me:

Sleep Deprivation/Night Sweats

Solutions

_1_   _Go to the doctors_

_2_   _Get into a day to day routine_

_3_   _Never sleep, take drugs to keep me awake_

_4_   _Become a vampire_

__Bulimia__ _(although fine now, could come back)_

Solutions

_1_   _Keep a regular eating pattern_

_2_   _Keep challenging food avoidances_

_3_   _Exercise_

_4_   _Get into a routine_

5	Let myself get ill again
6	Stop eating

Social Problems

Solutions

1. Keep in contact and start visiting friends

2. Make new relationships through a job

3. Make an effort to go out

4. Hide myself away

5. Isolate myself

6. Live forever as a crazy cat lady

Depression

Solutions

1	Go to the doctors to find the right medication
2	Stay with counseling
3	Confront issues straight away
4	Kill myself and make it all go away
5	Break my body so badly I can't function or take any control of my own life
6	Take control of my life

The lists went on and on until I no longer wanted to think anymore. After making short, medium and long term goals I fell asleep and only woke up once we pulled up outside their house in the middle of nowhere.

I was a zombie. I felt nothing anymore, nothing mattered. I watched mum make up my bed, changed into my pyjamas, cleaned my teeth and fell asleep praying that I would never ever wake up again.

Nine

December 2009

It's warm. The humidity is high but not
unbearable. The ground is hard but not
uncomfortable. My hands wander away from my
body; I brush the grass with my fingertips; cool,
moist. I'm having one of those rare moments
when I am so unbelievably content that I let my
mind wander. Its boxing day 2009. Only a few
months ago, I'm at the train station at Brisbane
central station. I'm nervous, it's been so long since
we saw each other. I was so worried that my
makeup was bad or my clothes looked too tight;
every stainless steel reflection I walked past I had
to check my hair. I stood at the gates of the station
scared that he would stand me up. A voice called
my name and as I turned I saw the same familiar
face that I had fallen in love with only a few years
ago. Blonde hair, gorgeous eyes and a smile that I
could bathe in. As he came towards me my heart
started beating faster, I ran towards him and
jumped into his arms that wrapped around me in
a familiar embrace that reminded me of meeting
him in the graveyard at home, half a world away,

and falling into his eyes. Things were different now; we had spent nearly a year apart and during that time I had to convince myself that he meant nothing to me, he had broken my heart once again and moved on. I had concentrated on losing weight and getting through sixth form and tried to forget. We were friends, that was all, that was all it ever could be.

We had met when I was just 15, I hadn't long moved from Cheltenham to Malvern and despite managing to make a lot of friends, I still found that my confidence was lacking. We met near the train station. I had gone to Cornwall with my best friend and bought a stick of rock for a guy I liked at the time, the guy acted like a dick in one way or another so I ended up throwing it at him as he came back from Worcester with a group of his friends. One of the friends in that group was Sam. From that moment on we started to get to know each other; we talked, we laughed, he'd walk me to hockey practice and back from school. There was a graveyard in between our houses which we'd often meet at and it became my favourite place in the world; it was there that I learnt about his family, what he loved to do. I listened to his music- Ocean Avenue by Yellow Card, I learnt the creases on his face when he smiled, memorized the way his mouth formed my name and how he loved to play.

After his girlfriend found out about me and I, in turn, found out about her, our relationship got complicated…I had death threats and calls from numbers I didn't recognise warning me that I needed to watch my back. Nothing had even happened with Sam and yet I still felt guilty because I had felt something for him before I knew that his girlfriend even existed, but for two days I watched my back. I had looked up who this girlfriend of his was and made every effort to avoid her. It came to a head after a couple of days; I was walking to the toilets before the school photos and as I was nearing the entrance I clocked her. She had her eyes set on my face and was making a beeline for me. I pushed my friends onwards, urging them to get through the toilet door but before I managed to get into what I thought would be safety, I felt a blinding pain in the back of my head. Harriet had pulled my hair back so hard that I had no choice but to change my course of movement.

She pushed me against the wall and started screaming, her words indecipherable apart from the odd "slut" "ugly" "fat" "bitch". My fight or flight failed to kick in and instead I started to try to reason with her, tell her that I never knew she was even with Sam and explain the situation, but after a minute or so she got tired of me, smashed my head against the wall and I fell to the ground. Needless to say my photo that year was not great. We clashed a few times after that; she decided she hated me, so for the first part of sixth form I was greeted with a barrage of insults every time I walked into the common room. If it wasn't for my amazing best friend Louise, it would have probably lasted longer.

After a million apologies from Sam I forgave him, and once the relationship between Sam and Harriet had ended we resumed our friendship, despite my head telling me to stop being an idiot. Harriet didn't like this turn of events however. The next time we were together was at a party; posh dresses, alcohol and a lot of music and dancing. It created the perfect opportunity for another fight. We ended up outside and I once again tried to explain and calm the situation down, despite knowing that all I wanted at that moment was to be with Sam. In between spats he comforted me which enraged her even more. It ended up with Lou stepping in and protecting me like no-one else ever has.

When Harriet called me a "fucking ginger slag", after trying to swing for me, Lou's retort was " you fucking what?" and hit her right back, something that we laughed a lot about afterwards – her wit showed in any situation.

She made sure Harriet didn't lay a finger on me for the rest of the night. I have never had anyone that has stuck up for me in that way before. I've never felt so grateful for a friend before that moment.

I spoke with Sam for most of the night despite him being the reason for the mess I was in. His touch made everything ok again and I came to the conclusion that I would walk through fire for him, for that smile and his laugh. When we were together he made me feel beautiful, when we were apart I couldn't stand my reflection.

For the next few years I kept him in my mind; loving him when he was there for me, wanting to hate him when he was with someone else, wishing I was good enough for him, wishing I was spectacular and beautiful, and everything else in between. We had been on and off for so long, I had convinced myself that I loved him, I wanted him to be the first but I had promised myself and in part my mother, that I wouldn't lose my virginity until I was sixteen. He was my one. I believed it with every inch of my being and that's all I allowed myself to know. He had the ability to make me fall for him over and over again. I hated and loved him for that.

Now things were different, we were 10317 miles away from the world we knew and we were friends. We were familiar faces in a strange part of the world. That day was one of the happiest of my life. I pried myself away from his embrace in the station and we continued on to talk about our experiences in Australia and explore Brisbane in the only way tourists know how. We walked along the town center, we took a boat ride which ended in me becoming unbelievably burnt, we talked about our experiences and travels over, we ate and we ended up watching the new Twilight film at the cinema (which I don't think either of us expected to watch that day). Once the film had ended and we stepped out into the afternoon light I realized I didn't want him to leave me. It had been so long since we had been able to laugh and be us that I craved more. As we walked back to the train station the decision to stop at the bars in the middle of the street was made. As always I was asked for ID, despite tiptoeing up when I got to the bar (my height never does me favours!). At the beginning we started with cocktails and then by the last bar we were watching football and drinking vodka pineapple. We decided to stay for the night, renting a bed in the hostel near the station, then deciding to go for a walk over the Brisbane bridge. Halfway over our conversation got interrupted.

As with most Australian downpours the rain came on suddenly: within minutes we were soaking wet. We ran and took shelter underneath the side of a clothing store, my hair was bedraggled and my makeup probably running. We laughed at the heavens opening above us and the fact that I was so wet through meant nothing. I turned and looked at him in those beautiful eyes of his and he murmured words that I'll never forget;

"You know what I've never done? I've never kissed you in the rain"

And with that he entwines his hands around my neck and pulls me closer to him, falling into the raindrops away from the shelter, his lips connecting with mine, reminding me of how much I was in love with him and how I would do anything for him. I am in heaven, I am in love.

The morning came too quickly; a moment of indescribable bliss came and went as quick as a racing car. We said goodbye, his lips once more pressing against mine and I believed that my life was sorted. I had found the man that I loved, the one that I wanted to be with and the person that could make me better.

My eyes open. Above me all there is is fire; thousands of galaxies burning bright above me and shining down on our tiny insignificant planet. My hands clutch the grass once again, remembering where I am. I am in Australia, I am alone and he is gone but I am having one of the most amazing experiences of my life. I am in the middle of nowhere with seven strangers and I've spent the night laughing. The sky is the most spectacular thing I have ever seen. The stars take my breath away and everything seems so vast and beautiful that I seem tiny and so insignificant. There is a canvas above me and it looks as if the sky can't fit into the space because the stars are filling it all up. I am in awe. I am in love. The world is beautiful.

Suddenly I feel scared. Something isn't right; I am alone and suddenly very afraid. Something beyond my vision is closing in on me and I know that I am in danger. It's too hot and I can't protect myself. I need to disappear fast but I don't know how. It's too hot. I can't breathe.

I woke up sweating in the Abbey once more.

Ten

2012

Waking up soaking again was the last thing that I wanted.

After my night in Marc's room I had hardly slept. We had swapped numbers and once in our own rooms began a frantic texting session that did nothing to calm me down or ready me for sleep. The uncomfortable night sweats made everything so much worse, so by the time I needed to be up I was exhausted. Working out that I had enough time to go and smoke before I was allowed a shower, I threw on some clean clothes, a big jumper and my slippers. The cold slammed into my face as I went outside to the smoking area. The air was fresh and clean, the sun was beginning to rise painting the sky with a beautiful pastel blue.

I have an obsession with sky; the way that the clouds constantly move and collide into one another, their beautiful ever changing patterns and pictures that they create- the depth they exhibit fascinating the eye with a distance far too big to contemplate. The colours; blues, pinks, purples, greens, oranges, reds. So unbelievably beautiful and powerful that a simple sunrise can take my breath away and a sunset renders me speechless. I love the sky. It seems so infinite, so amazing that I could stare up for hours. When I was ill and isolated I would just sit on my bed and watch the day change; from morning til night it was just me and the sky. I wished that I could become part of it and be something so spectacular that people could fall in love with it in the same way that I had.

Sitting down on the plastic green chair and wrapping myself up away from the chill, I savoured the only time that I would spend on my own for the rest of the day. The door opened and out came of one the other ED girls, Bella, we lived close to one another but were completely different in so many ways. Bella was tall, ghostly pale and had become so thin that her eyes seemed to protrude out of her skull, her short hair style accentuated her jaw line - she was a cartoon character and, before I got to know her, she had petrified me. Every other word was "fuck". Her attitude towards the staff at The Abbey was sometimes so vulgar it made no sense to me. She was on her second or third admission in the space of a year so she knew the staff well - this she used to her advantage and would often get away with murder but her humour was quite funny and she was actually very loving after you break through the anger. She had already tried to run away once during my stay. She got as far as the bus stop before they caught up with her, and I had come out of the ED lounge to see her being dragged back into the hallway. She looked like she had collapsed. Bella had a dark past, littered with abuse. She seemed to have learnt that she was her only friend in the world - trust was hard and she'd never talk about her family unless we were alone. It made me sad to think that not everyone had the same supportive family that I did, but hers seemed toxic and I didn't blame her for wanting to get away.

We sat in silence, just smoking, no words were needed in the morning; you need the time to prepare yourself for the day ahead and the food you're going to have to endure.

I finished my cigarette and said a quick "see you later". My date with the sunrise was over and it was time for another day. After a quick shower and deciding that maybe, just this once, I should make an effort and put some makeup on, it was time to meet the rest of the ED lot and head for breakfast. As always we were escorted into the dining hall; such a grand room in such a grand building but unbelievably depressing. Not only are we force fed in this room it's decor is less than appealing. The room is littered with tiny tables covered with boring tablecloths and oversized silver cutlery. I always ate faster than the anorexics because I was used to pretending that eating wasn't a problem for me so I would eat at a normal pace but then purge after at moment I could. They however, couldn't pretend. Karen would eat so slowly and often break apart during meals, other girls would cut everything into the size of a pea before it entered their mouth, some would take nearly an hour to eat a main meal and that was even before they were served the compulsory dessert. Finishing first made me feel fatter, greedier and although I knew it was unhealthy and wrong I would try to slow down to a snails pace so I wasn't left out. Mostly however I was left to stare at the room; the imperfections in the walls, noticing the fact that there were way too many lights in the room. I often sat for ages counting them all and really wondering what their electric bill for this one singular room would be. There were lights on the walls and all over the ceiling - There was over twenty...Twenty lights for one room? Slightly excessive if you ask me.

So many of my meals were spent contemplating the lights; some days it would really aggravate me and some days it would make me want to laugh. I think I was trying to distract myself from all the food I was loading into my body. After a few days at the Abbey I was eating more than I ever had; 3 large meals, 3 snacks (that usually included chocolate), a dessert after dinner and a Fortisip, that made me want to hurt whoever gave it to me by throwing the bottle at their head.

My light counting was interrupted by Mabel - the overweight waitress clearing my bowl,

"Alright my lover?" she said in her thick Bristolian accent.

She was the brightness to everyones morning, despite the fact that she brought you the thing you wanted the least.

Once breakfast was done we were sent back to our lounge to suffer the consequences. During the day I had no choice but to sleep or distract myself and count down to the time that I could get the hell out of there. I began to draw again, to while away the hours, I had always loved it but, because I wasn't very good I stopped after A-Level: being marked and getting a D kind of ruined the passion I found within it. Why spend your life failing at something? I drew my friends, I drew Sam (big mistake as I cried for an hour afterwards) I drew birds. Anything that could distract me for half an hour I'd attempt.

The time came where we were freed and I met Marc in the ATP lounge. He sat with David and Richard, two alcoholics who had come to try and banish the wine bottle from their lives. I learnt so much about them that night, they were married and still in love. They had good jobs and good homes. Patrick worked in aviation and had a brilliant mind and David had a laugh that made even the worst day feel okay. They were explaining to Marc and I about the injections they have to get to help them with any withdrawal symptoms. Nothing about these shots made them appealing. Not only were they in your arse but they apparently hurt like a motherfucker; you could tell when someone had one as they'd struggle with sitting down for the next couple of days. In turn I taught them all how to play shithead, a card game that I had spent most of sixth form playing and the only one that I could ever remember how to play. We spent the evening chatting, laughing and playing shithead, I almost forgot that I was in a hospital for the mentally ill and full of addicts. There are always moments of brightness in the darkest of places and it's usually because of the people around you. I had such an opinion on alcoholics before I went into The Abbey, I soon found it was completely misguided and wrong; I thought that they just sat at home drinking, angry, abusive. Until then the only people that I had known with alcohol problems were members of my family that we had distanced ourselves from. These men were so different; successful business men, husbands, kind and so much fun to be around. My narrow-minded views were shot to pieces.

At that moment there was a commotion outside; stern voices and a voice to the reception desk telling them to call the police. We were told to stay in the lounge as the police arrived and later on discovered that the man who slept in the room next to me had a knife and he wasn't willing to give it up. I hadn't liked him from the minute I saw him, and word soon got around that he was a sex addict. Patients saw him with his hands down his trousers at the dinner table, he was always walking around with his belt undone and his general demeanour was frightening. He was on 24 hour supervision which meant he was watched constantly; going to the loo, eating, bathing, anytime he moved someone was there watching. A high risk patient.We were allowed back to our rooms once the police had arrived and the night ended with me sat in my room hearing the man try to reason with the staff and the officers; he insisted that he didn't need to be in this place, that he was a professional hypnotherapist and he had a life that he just wanted to live. Instead of making me feel sorry for him I just felt more scared.

That man could hypnotize people!?

He could get into peoples heads and yet couldn't keep his hands out of his pants?

Now I had seen a lot of crazy shit in this place but this was too far even for me to accept. The knife was taken eventually without too much hassle.

After that and he calmed down and returned to his room but, despite having someone there watching him, I didn't sleep much that night.

Eleven

2012

During my time at The Abbey I had various visits
from my family. One afternoon my oldest sister,
Ella, brought her youngest daughter who's little
giggle took my mind off everything that was
tearing me up. She also reminded me, on a day
when all I wanted to do was die and get away
from what I was being forced to go through, that I
had a reason to live and I had a reason to get
better and be an example for my nieces and
nephews when they were growing up. I had a
family that loved me. I didn't want to be the
daughter, the sister or the auntie that they never
got to know because she couldn't escape her
demons.

Another night my Mum and my step dad, Joe,
came to visit. It had been a horrible day and all I
wanted to do was cry but again I put on a brave
face for them. The visit soon turned sour when
one of the staff made a mistake and left the
bathroom key in my door. Just before Mum and

Joe left I noticed the key in the lock. My heart soared. I'm not sure if I was excited about the fact that I could finally pee without anyone watching or that if I wanted to throw up I could, but before I knew it Mum had taken the key and was going to give it back to reception. This wasn't fair. I was so full.

I tried to reason with her, "It's fine Mum, I'm not going to be sick. You can leave it there, I'll take it back after you've left"

"No i'm taking back to the reception Emily" she said holding my freedom in her hand.

I begged and pleaded but she didn't give in. I hated her in that moment, I hated that she was stopping me from feeling better, that she was leaving me to feel sick and bloated and fat. So I did what any petulant child would do and called her a 'douche'-they left without saying goodbye.

I was never able to swear at my mum no matter how annoyed I was. Calling her a 'douche' was probably the worst thing that I could have got away with.   I was ashamed, angry and upset that I had let them leave on bad terms, that I was so angry at her, that I hadn't said sorry, that I was acting like a child. I fumed for about an hour and I near enough regressed into being 5 years old again; I wanted to scream but instead paced the floor, hit myself in the face and tore at my body with my nails until tears filled my eyes. I didn't want to be recovered if it meant this thick, suffocating weight had to be on me, but I didn't want to die. I was in a state of limbo and didn't know what to do or how to feel anymore.

There was a cup on the side.

I was fed up of feeling fat, ugly and full. I didn't care anymore; I didn't care about the stupid rules in this place; I didn't care about whether I lived or died.

I wanted to die.

Screw it all, I didn't care.

A moment of weakness. I grabbed the cup and without thinking, threw up into it. The relief washed over me like a wave. It was as if all the anger and tension I felt was instantly released from my diaphragm.

I was still full though, a cup was a lot smaller than my stomach now.

What had I done?

What do I do now?

The windows in The Abbey didn't open properly. They were limited to a couple of inches so that people couldn't escape.

I had to get rid of the evidence.

I was pretty sure I would be asked to leave if anyone found out…did I want to leave?

The reality of one stupid moment in time had started to set in. I was an idiot.

The relief washed away and in its place came a wave of guilt which pummelled me with its dark force. I poured what was in the cup out of the crack that the window would allow and used water from another cup to wash it out. All the time expecting someone to walk in and catch me in the act.

Why was I incapable of this?

Why did my emotions control me so much?

I was risking my recovery because I had gotten angry. I was pushing back against everyone trying to help me. I was a failure. I crawled into my bed, exhausted from the abuse I had just instilled on my body; my stomach bleeding from the scratches, my face pulsating from the punches. The pins and needles were back- the pins and needles that liked to remind me that my potassium levels were low and barely keeping my muscles functioning anymore. The potassium levels that meant I could be one purge from death if my heart gave out. The levels that had nearly killed me. I lay there; my hands exploring my shoulders, my ribs, my waist. Body checking, comfort - all they found was skin. I couldn't feel my bones anymore, it was official; I was a fat failure.

I was nothing.

I was worth nothing.

The next morning I woke up, though you could hardly call what happened to me that night sleep. It was weigh day and I was petrified. Over my time in The Abbey I had eaten and kept down more food than I had in the past year, if not longer. My brain had been fried with all the evil thoughts that my eating disorder instilled in me. I wanted to shut off my thoughts for just one second, escape the constant battle between staying still and moving forwards. I didn't know what I thought or who I was anymore. It was safe being ill - I knew what to expect. Getting better was journeying into the unknown.

I dragged myself outside for another cigarette to try and calm me down. I sat there and tried to distract myself from thoughts of large numbers and breaking the scale. There was no beautiful sunrise to greet me this time, rainy greyness surrounded me, perfectly reflecting my mood. I forced myself to concentrate on the cigarette I was lighting. I suddenly realised that the only way in which I could be on my own or get out of the ED lounge during the day was to smoke, I had nearly got through 100 already- I had only been there for about 4 days. (During my time there I must have smoked in total between 200-300 cigarettes) I had never smoked that much before. It was like I was rebelling against getting better by clogging up my lungs. Attempting to go from one addiction to another.

It was disgusting but I had to die somehow, right?

Weigh in was a nightmare. Having to strip off in front of someone was bad enough; the fear, the judgement, the embarrassment - stepping on the scale and not being able to look at the number almost gave me a breakdown. I needed to know how much I had gained. I needed the knowledge, the control; anything was better than what was going on in my head.

I started to cry and once I started I couldn't stop.

I couldn't cope inside my body or my mind. I felt like I could feel the fat cascading off me; rolls of fat rubbing against each other and splurging out of my underwear. I was the most disgusting thing I had ever seen. My eating disorder had infected my brain and caused my eyes to see something completely different to what others did. But I believed the lies; they were truth to me: I couldn't look any uglier in this moment than now.

In a trance I put my clothes back on, not hearing anything that the nurse said - just registering the look of concern on her face.I dragged myself down the corridor, seeing nothing and only feeling fat, then heaved myself into the shower. My tears were drowned by the cascading water. My fingers wove through my hair, pulling at the knots and tearing the strands from my scalp. Enjoying the release the pain gave me. I grabbed at my body for bones I couldn't feel anymore. Looking for the comfort and finding none. There was nothing left to comfort me now. The doctors, nurses, dieticians and my family were ruining everything, taking all of my coping mechanisms away from me.

Once clean and changed, I began to try and put some make up on using the distorted mirror in my room in an attempt to hide my red, tired eyes. In my eyes, giving people with body dysmorphia distorted mirrors was a really stupid idea. What I had in my head was torture; seeing myself in a circus mirror was even more confusing and frustrating. There was a knock on the door.

Glancing at my phone to check that I wasn't late for breakfast, I whispered "Come in".

The dietician walked through my door before I even finished my sentence. "Can we talk?" Her tone had a hint of something I couldn't recognise.

She sat on my bed without invitation and I was suddenly afraid that they had found out what I had done. I stayed away from her and sat in one of the chairs, fists clenched, stomach dropping, adrenaline racing. She proceeded to tell me that they had to do something about the amount I was eating. I prayed that they were going to reduce my meals - that they had realised I didn't need as much as they were giving me and the constant feeding would stop.

But no, my weight had gone down. They were upping my snacks and introducing another dreaded Fortisip.

I think my exact words were: "Are you fucking kidding me?"

I'm not usually downright rude but this little nugget of information was too much for my brain to process politely.

HOW had my weight gone down?

DOWN?

This had to be some sort of joke. Some kind of fucked up test they were doing on me. I was hardly coping. I was eating a ridiculous amount and they wanted to force in more?!

How could I do it without exploding? My stomach already felt at breaking point. It was torture.

One tiny slip up wouldn't have changed my weight. I knew that, didn't I? I hadn't done any exercise, apart from a few sit ups in my room after hours - hell, I was hardly even allowed to walk around without feeling as though one of the nurses were silently counting my steps, but from what the dietician was saying, it had dropped a significant amount. Enough for them to be worried. They needed my weight to be going up and the only way that they could do this was to up my already huge calorie intake - which was more than a normal adults as it was.

I needed them to fuck right off.

I needed everything to stop. For everyone to give up on me and leave me alone. I was convinced they were lying to me.

The reality of it, which perhaps deep down I knew but didn't want to believe, was that because they had got me eating properly and I had no choice but to keep it down, my body had been kick-started again and my metabolism had sped up. There's no doubt that the amount of food that anorexics and bulimics have to eat during treatment leaves them feeling uncomfortable, bloated and "fat", and even in physical pain, but with determination and a hell of a lot of inner strength their bodies will adapt, get used to it and start to function normally again.

The body is an amazing thing. The problem however, is that your mind never shuts up throughout the process and refuses to believe the logic: Every time you pick up a fork or sit down for a meal all you can hear is that familiar voice; "you don't need that fatty", "you are ugly and fat enough already", "you don't deserve this", "you're a horrible human being", "no one likes you", "you don't deserve to be alive": endless insults swarming your mind. Most can't get past the beginning stage of re-feeding and give into the disordered thoughts, taking steps back to ruin their recovery, delving them further into illness and each time you dip it's harder to get back out..

The dietician left me feeling confused, betrayed and angry. The day ahead had got a whole lot scarier now and I just wanted to go back to bed and ignore it. No such luck; it was time for breakfast and time to face my fears.

Jesus.

I sat there at breakfast counting. I sat there at lunch counting. I sat there at dinner counting. Trying to distract myself from the impossibility of what had happened that morning. Not counting calories but the hours in which I had wasted my life…One binge could be as little as 20 minutes to 8 hours. I never had a day off. If I averaged that every day that was….man I was terrible at maths…so say 4 hours a day….that was 1,460 hours a year….that was 24-ish days a year, 511 days….that was nearly 2 years. Wasted. I had spent hours and hours of my life, being sick - I hadn't even added in all the time I had spent worrying about how fat I was, the minutes wasted staring in the mirror hating myself. The time had slyly slipped past me. I'd frittered away 2 years of my life just on being sick. It seemed insane.

All these numbers that I couldn't fathom: Nearly six stone. The potassium levels of someone that was near death. The depression score that was one of the worst that my doctor had seen in someone my age. Why was it that the numbers that I cared about in my life were the ones that in the grand scheme of things meant nothing? I hadn't cared about test scores or how many things I had achieved, instead I chased lower numbers on the scale, counted the number of ribs I could feel - constantly feeding the thing that was killing me. Constantly falling and then there it was, meal number one of the day. Endless numbers, endless calories, endless thoughts and fears.

I picked up my fork ready for the facade that I could normally portray; pretending I was fine, pretending that I could be normal. But for the first time during my stay there, I couldn't face it. I wanted to push the food off my plate; colouring the tablecloth with stinking slop and fat. No part of me wanted to eat. I just sat there staring, getting angrier and angrier at the food in front of me. Knowing full well that this wasn't me, this was my disorder, but I didn't care. It could take hold of me, it could take my life. I was done. Without a future to worry about I was free. There'd be no more counting, no more feeling guilty, no more hating myself. I could be peaceful and feel nothing. Screw food, screw my disgusting body, and screw everything.

My protest wasn't allowed to last long. Eyes were on me, always on me. I realised I could never win against the staff there. After an hour, once all the other patients had left, I had to give in. That night I ate cold slush. What it was I can't even remember. My only memory was hating every single mouthful. My insistence to not being treated like a child had backfired and instead I had digressed into a childlike state; needing to be coaxed, needing to be cared for and needing to be told what I had to do.

I hated myself that day. I hated my eating disorder. I even hated everyone around me; after all, if none of my family cared I could die and they'd be a hell of a lot better off without me.

Why couldn't they see that when it was so

blatantly obvious?

Why couldn't they let me go?

Why couldn't they let me die?

I was nothing but bad news and more problems. The same old thoughts hovered in my head. Why did they care? How could they when I was such a waste of space? I wasn't good enough. I fell asleep that night and dreamt of nothing but my gravestone. I'd dream of it at least twice a week at this point. Different scenarios every time; people crying, people facing away, an empty plot with an old boot to mark that someone was buried there. I used to plan my funeral in my head all the time; what songs would play, who I'd want to come, what I'd want them to say. I woke up feeling desolate and lost, unable to see how I could move on from this or how I could get better. I was sure that I was going to die from this illness and I wanted it to be soon. I was tired of fighting.

Little did I know that that day would be the one in which I would have to face some home truths and admit things to myself that meant I would finally begin to detach myself from the comfort blanket of my eating disorder. The eating disorder that had smothered me for so many years and ruined my life.

Twelve

2012

Monday 29th October

I'm struggling.

I feel so low, so empty and depressed. I'm not in control of my eating disorder in the slightest. It's like I'm filling my life with excuses and lies. Mum keeps promising me things will get better but I just can't see how they possibly can. I'm scared and anxious about so many things. Having to pay rent and bills is terrifying and I'm not sure why. Living in the Forest of Dean and working in Cheltenham can't work forever either; my money is going down the drain with fuel, food and my fucking eating disorder. I don't feel ready for anything but staying where I am is equally as traumatic. I don't know what I'm doing anymore or where I want to go.

I think that's maybe why the prospect of death is so attractive, I feel like I'm failing in life and I'm scared to fall.

Sam has appeared back in my life, he's an emotional wreck after breaking up with his girlfriend and as hard as I try not to care about him, I wish I could make things better. I also wish he could make me better...I'm scared how much longer I'll be like this."

…Two weeks later I was in hospital.

Thirteen

2012

The morning after weigh day I woke up and for a few seconds I forgot everything; I forgot that I was in a hospital for people with addictions and mental health problems. I forgot that I could die at any moment. I forgot about Sam and my lack of friends, the failure in my dream of becoming an actress, but most of all, that Nanny wasn't there to hold me anymore and tell me I was going to be alright. Remembering Nanny was always hard; whether it be her laugh, the way that she used to cook enough to feed the 5,000 every Sunday just so our family could all be together, the way she used to go for her little jogs around the living room to keep fit when she was diagnosed. The way her face looked after she died as I lay with her stroking her short hair, lost by the chemo. I remembered it all and my life over the last few years was brought back to me. She'd be so disappointed in me and so upset that I couldn't seem to fight this off. I missed her so much it felt like there was a constant hole in my heart but I was thankful that she never had to see me like this.

I dragged myself out of bed and peeled my soaking clothes off my body to change into something that wasn't freezing. We had a few hours till we could shower and have breakfast so once again it was cigarette time. Outside I bumped into Marc and immediately regretted not wearing any makeup. Say hello to first thing in the morning face! We sat for a while and smoked and talked. It was so refreshing to talk to someone that made your heart race, someone who could accept whatever you told them and made you feel comfortable and unafraid. We had both had a speaking to since the night in his room. Sue, one of the key workers there, had taken me into my room and once again explained that patient relationships were strictly forbidden. She then went on to tell me that I can't find my self-esteem in other people and that Marc needed to concentrate on why he was there too. He had only told me as much as he wanted to and had a lot of problems to deal with. Even after those words of warning though, I completely ignored her. I respected the no patient relationships….I mean it wasn't as though Marc and I were going to share a romantic meal together in the dining room, then let hormones invade us and frisk each other on the tablecloth surrounded by sex addicts, manic depressives and the eating disorder patients…although at times it was very tempting. I knew that we had to just be friends and I was absolutely fine with that. Their logic made sense but the problem was that every moment Marc and I had the chance to talk, we were whisked away from each other or warned once more. It frustrated the hell out of me. That morning though we were free to chat completely uninterrupted and it felt refreshing. He took my head away from the sadness I had felt when I woke up and it revitalised me. Just his presence seemed to prep me for the day ahead.

After yet another breakfast of toast, bran flakes and counting lights I returned to the lounge for my first Fortisip of the day, I was once again faced with the usual dilemma of throw and go (the thought of chucking the shake at the nearest persons head and doing one for the door) or just down and deal with it. Trying not to be a problem patient, I chose the latter. My weight loss was still playing on my mind, but not as much as the amount of food I was going to have to pile into my body.

I was ready to spend the day feeling fat. I knew I'd spend the day feeling fat. During treatment certain phrases circle round in your head, one of which is "fat isn't a feeling". Which technically is true but it still used to frustrate the hell out of me.

When you are feeling "fat" you can be feeling a multitude of different things; sad, happy, angry, hungry, full, confused, nervous, neglected, afraid, alone, unsatisfied. So many different emotions can confuse you and instead of identifying what your problems actually are you collect them all together and label it as 'fat' just because it's easier. Think about it, how many times do you look at yourself and think "I feel fat" when actually the root of your emotions is some completely different problem. You could be feeling anxious, helpless, stressed, sad, worried, a multitude of emotions that you just can't handle. However the day took a turn that I completely didn't expect. It was a day of learning about other people and I forgot about myself which was surprisingly refreshing.

Sat in the ED lounge with the girls - Gemma, Sophie (a gorgeous Welsh girl who was slightly younger than I was), one of the younger staff members and Fiona. Fiona wasn't technically meant to be in with us as she was on the mental health ward but because everyone loved her she got away with everything! I wasn't sure what Fiona suffered, all I knew is that she'd be in the middle of a conversation with you and start muttering to herself then snap back into the conversation just as quickly as her mind had left. She'd also burst out into a loud laugh every now and then which was unbelievably infectious. At times she was slightly childlike which made you want to give her a cuddle and protect her. Most patients are quite scared of her at first but once they understand her and get to know her better they love her just like everyone else. We sat in the lounge talking properly for the first time. I hadn't heard some of the girls laugh until today. Gemma was talking about her brother's hairstyle but instead of calling it a "quiff" she described it as a "queef". Cue Sophie and me looking at each other in confusion, as Sophie explained to Gemma that she was pretty sure that a "queef" meant something else and Gemma battled back saying her brother definitely had a "queef" I got my iPhone out and googled. Yep, it was as I thought. A "queef" is a slang word for "fanny fart". We broke apart laughing, I hadn't cried with laughter for years and it felt so amazing to just let go and enjoy a moment of complete joy. One of the staff from reception even came to see what all the noise was about, Fiona just sat there with no clue what we were on about. When we finally found the air to tell her she looked both horrified and humoured and then announced that she'd have to tell her sons when they came to visit. As we carried on chuckling away Fiona then started to tell us, in her way (which involved a lot of inward talking and loud bursts of laughter) that she never got told about sex and she thought babies would come from a mole in her arm but she made sure, she said as she waggled her finger and her head waggled slightly with it, she made sure that her sons knew "your father put it in there! HA!". We were all amazed and utterly amused; my stomach was killing but this time instead of it being because of food, it was because I actually was enjoying myself. The good humour lasted till we got to dinner and as we sat on our usual table, we heard Fiona loudly telling the Addiction Treatment Patients about it. Marc's half horrified and half amused face definitely brightened up my day. We giggled till dessert.

That evening Karen announced that she was leaving, I was sad to see her go as she was so kind but I knew that she wasn't coping. Every mealtime she struggled. Every bite tortured her and she told me that she doesn't feel like her body deserves nourishment or any good to be put in it. She had been trying to fight it for her daughters and her husband, but you can't recover for other people. You have to identify that you are worth recovery. Anorexia is a terrible illness; it tears people's souls in two. I found out not long after I left that she had died.Like so many others that I had met, she was unable to deal with her demons and her illness had taken everything from her..and her family.

The last of the evening was spent once again in the ATP (Addiction Treatment Patients) lounge with the guys, laughing about the events of the last few days and once again being surprised about what people say. One of the new patients on the program was Delilah and she'd spent the day reading out letters from two of the closest people in her life, which is a stage in the recovery process. They write to you and tell you how the alcohol addiction had affected them. As a patient you have the capability to see someone else's point of view. Delilah was a blonde bombshell in her 40's. When she wasn't being shy she had a good sense of humour but she was tainted with a seriousness that her life has instilled in her. She read the letters to me. She'd had a hard life; losing a baby, then being made redundant, which spurred on her alcohol addiction and resulted in her husband leaving her. Marc told me later that she drove her car off a cliff when she got really bad: if she had been wearing a seatbelt she would have certainly died, but instead she was thrown from her convertible and landed on the beach. It was unbelievable to hear and suddenly I realised that people that go through stuff still manage to live. It was so obvious - so confusing but so simple at the same time!

There were so many people that had gone through worse than I had and yet here I was letting life defeat me, letting myself get hit repeatedly and now refusing to stand up again.

You have to force yourself through every single day sometimes. You have to fight for the people you love, you have to work hard these days to live a comfortable life and work towards bettering yourself and who you are every single day. You aren't stuck with life if you work with yourself and for yourself. You can live with *life*, and happily at that. I understood that my recovery wasn't just going to happen if I waded through the motions; I had to work and work hard. If I actually wanted to live then it was time to start fighting.

Once the men from the addiction treatment

program reappeared the conversation quickly turned back to a less serious topic: can you die from too much masturbation? It took me a while to stop laughing and get rid of David and Richards voices in my head; wondering how the sex addict had smuggled the knife in, Richard saying "I wonder if he had put it up his bum?" to which David gave us a wicked look and replied "double pleasure".

Fourteen

2012

The next day I had another lecture off the nurse about Marc. They had been watching us like hawks and weren't comfortable with us spending time together even though we were rarely alone. It frustrated me that the staff seemed to be making our friendship a massive deal when nothing had even happened between us, sure we laughed together, talked about our problems and comforted each other on hard days, but that's what friends are for and at that moment in my life all I needed was a friend.

I spent the time before breakfast drawing and filling in my learning portfolio, every patient had one, it was full of questions and we were required to answer every single one; pages and pages of questions that I didn't want to answer.

1.Feeling Fat – What does it feel like? How do I feel?

"Like I'm completely out of proportion, I'm so aware of my body, of my stomach and how it feels flabby when I even just sit

doing nothing. I look in the mirror and I'm so disappointed with my reflection and feel so low in myself, I have images in my head of what I SHOULD look like, it's quite hard to even just be on my own because I feel like my body is just so repulsive. As a result, I feel very low and disappointed with myself. I get angry with how negatively I think and constantly call myself pathetic. I also think I'm very unappealing and ugly."

2. My Illness- What do I like most about it? What do I dislike most about it? Do I want to give it up? Do I want to hold on to it?

"I like that I know how to use it to my advantage to get thinner, I like the satisfaction it gives me and the control I have.

-I hate that I'm getting weaker and my social life is practically non-existent, I hate that I can't get away from it and it's a complete part of me.

-To an extent I do want to get rid of it but I don't want to get bigger.

-Partly. Yes I want to keep it. I don't know"

After filling in a few pages I was mentally exhausted, I didn't like thinking about myself, I didn't feel as though I was myself and instead the only thing that was defining me was my illness. I was an empty shell of a person and worth nothing.

I was called in for another weigh in and blood test to check my potassium levels, so I dragged myself off the sofa and into the doctor's room. Once again I had to strip off and step on those dreaded scales. I stood there half naked praying, my eyes tightly shut and muscles tensed against the chill in the room. After I stepped off they told me my weight had gone up but wouldn't say any more. Thoughts crashed around my head; how much had I gained weight? Was it a lot? Was I now getting too big? Did this mean they'd take me off all the extra food? My inner monologue was interrupted when I was asked to lie down on the examining table for bloods. The nurse spent the next ten minutes stabbing in my arms, fruitlessly trying to find blood and suddenly my brain reminded me of the only real hospital admission I'd ever had before The Abbey...

It was in the summer before sixth form and I had gone to Turkey with my mum and some family friends. Back then things were different as mum was still single and I was quickly falling for Sam. I'd spent the holiday worrying about what food was on my plate as being in a bikini made me want to cry. In my eyes I was pale and flabby and disgusting. The day before we left, the others went on a boat ride and I had stayed behind with mum as I was getting really bad cramps. After a few hours the pain was unbearable and I could hardly move. Mum somehow found a man that took us to the doctor's surgery and from there I was quickly rushed to hospital with suspected appendicitis. We were in a foreign country where no one spoke English and because time was short, we had no choice but to go to the local hospital to try and find out exactly what was wrong. Memories blurred in and out; stained bed sheets, filthy floors, a woman crying. My mums face looking scared. Why did she look scared? They suspected that my appendix had burst and they only had a very short time period before it went from life threatening to critical. My mother's hands helped to dress me in a gown and my self-consciousness managed to lift its head out of the pain and made sure I asked her to tie it up tight so no one saw my bum. Not only did they make me wear crocs but they also forced me to walk to put them on, forever instilling in me a hatred for those awful looking, "pointless shoes"…And then I was lying on the operating table. Men in masks looked down at me with dark eyes. They grabbed my arms and legs and strapped them down. They took off my gown leaving me lying naked and unable to move. I looked around for my mum to comfort me and tell me that what they were doing was ok. But I was alone. Then the surgeon started prepping his instruments and for a wild moment of panic I thought that they were just going to cut me open right there without bothering to sedate me first. "What's your brother's name?" said a man as he pushed a large silver needle in my arm "Simon" I whispered out loud. Then my brain kicked in "What a stupid question to ask someone when you're putting them to sleep! What an absolute berk. Has he never watched TV? Surely they should be making me count to twenty or something?" and with that I fell asleep.

When I woke up I was lying in the same ward that I had been positioned in when I was admitted. I saw my mother's face and started crying because I was awake and I was alive. I asked for Louise and Sam, then I threw up. I have no idea how long I was in that hospital. It may have only been another day or it could have been as long as three. All I know is that mum made sure I was out of there as soon as possible before I caught something. The whole hospital was like something out of a news report or movie; the ward was just one big room with dark walls, the floors were filthy and my bed sheets looked like they hadn't been changed in a long time. Mum was training to be a midwife at the time and had spent her time waiting for me talking to the other patients and checking out the facilities. She was shocked to find that the birthing unit was one tiny room with five beds packed into it and 3 women giving birth at the same time. The sheets from those births would then be dumped in the ladies toilets which themselves were just a hole in the ground covered in excrement and god knows what else. The woman a few beds up from mine had cancer and at one point her catheter bag fell on the dirty, stained floor, perfect for any infections to jump into and travel into her frail body. Mum tried for ages to find a nurse to change it but as your family members have to look after you in hospital, the nurse just picked it off the floor and hung it back up again. There was no hope in this hospital. Everything was dark, dingy and depressing.

"Got it!" exclaimed the nurse, I brought myself back to The Abbey and quickly looked around, checking that the room was clean and blood stain free. I looked down and as the vial filled up with dark liquid, part of me wanted to say "well done, you can actually do your job" but I bit my tongue and just amused myself with my sarcasm. I'd get the results the next day, so all there was to do now was to see if I could persuade someone to take me outside for a cigarette and waste time for the rest of the day. After getting one of the younger and much more understanding members of the staff team to take me outside, I lit a Marlborough and text Marc

"Remembered something really weird today. Had weigh day as well, my weight has gone up :/ Can we meet tonight in the ATP Lounge"?

It was freezing; I was starting to wish I'd brought gloves with me. How had this year gone by so fast? How much weight had I gained? My phone vibrated a reply "I'm having a nightmare day too, Delilah is doing my head in. Yeah sure meet me when you've been freed!xx"

That evening at 9o'clock I walked into the ATP lounge expecting to see Marc's face, but it was empty.

I got a text "I'll be 20 minutes late" I knew he was on a home visit for the day so I sat with one of my fellow ED patients, Bella, and chatted instead. An hour later he wasn't back and wasn't answering any of the texts I sent him. I started to worry, this was not like him, and anyway, he wasn't allowed to go on home visits yet so where was he? By half past eleven I was debating whether to tell the staff; I knew they should probably be aware that one of their patients was MIA but I didn't want to have to tell them that we were texting, as I was pretty sure that wouldn't be allowed.

But then I got another message through on my phone which made me heart sink; "I've relapsed. I'm so ashamed of myself. It's so hard.x"

Try as I may I couldn't encourage him to come back, so after a cigarette with Bella and trying to slyly call him, I went up to the front desk and told them what I knew. I was sent to my room after being assured they were in contact with his Dad who was trying to get him to come back to The Abbey and back into treatment.

I spent most of the night worrying. I think that I would have with anyone that I knew there. There is camaraderie when you are in places such as The Abbey; people that you wouldn't necessarily be friends with become your best friends because you are going through the same things. But most of those relationships you build up don't last in the real world.

It's like if you were stuck on an airplane

nose-diving into the sea; the person that sat across from you who you'd been having a chat with would become your soul mate because you're both filled with fear and you want to be there for each other in your final moments. The guy who you sat next to who you thought smelt a bit funny and had weird hair suddenly becomes the love of your life because you don't want to die alone. Then the airplane somehow recovers and doesn't crash and when you get back home, the lifelong friendship and the all-time love that you found on the plane soon faces reality; the guy really does smell quite bad and the girl you sat holding hands with is actually a massive bitch. Everyone in treatment feels like they are going down into an abyss. You need support from other people, support from 'friends' and you vow that you'll be friends forever. It's a brilliant thing to have at the time, but once you are in recovery and back in the real world, you realise that some of those friendships you make are actually toxic for you. Instead of having a friendship that benefits you both it's actually doing more harm than good.

Marc didn't feel like a treatment friend though, there was something more to him. Something that I hadn't quite discovered yet but was desperate to. I lay there thinking about him till I fell asleep but it wasn't until the next day when I saw him that I finally let myself relax in the knowledge that he was okay and I wasn't going to lose him just yet.

The end of my time in The Abbey was approaching. After Marc's relapse we spoke a lot more about seeing each other in the real world. I'd visit him in Cardiff and he'd come to the Forest Of Dean, where my mum lived. I knew I should be concentrating on myself, what I was going to do and how I was going to manage, but around him I was like a schoolgirl; giggling and blushing, the outside world forgotten as I became caught up in the electricity between us.

I started going to groups during the day which meant my days sped by faster. My first group session was labelled 'managing emotions' and a couple of the ED girls along with one woman I'd never seen before traipsed up to the room. We sat in moss green high backed armchairs which smelled slightly of mildew and coffee. They were huge, so I could wriggle into a ball and get comfortable as though protecting myself from whatever I would have to face in this session. As I looked at the familiar faces of the girls that I had come to know, my eyes rested on the new woman who I didn't recognise. She was short, maybe in her fifties and wore clothes that made me think she'd just come from clearing out some stables. Her green jumper was faded and dull, blending in with the chair behind her, the beige combats draped around her legs did little for her figure and her hair was frizzy and wild. She looked tired. Then she turned and looked me straight in the face, obviously aware that I was staring at her. I changed to look at my feet so as not to be rude, the pain and the sadness that I had just felt in her from one flicker of eye contact made me uncomfortable. I could tell from that one look that the story of this woman was not a happy one. The class went off without a hitch, but I couldn't get this woman's face out of my head. I later found out that she had been part of the Special Forces and had been through very hard operations in Kosovo and the Middle East. She never spoke but there were rumours about her whole regiment being killed apart from her and one other friend, right in front of her eyes. She made me feel bad, guilty almost, as the reasons that she was in there weren't her fault at all, whereas I felt that with my admission I was completely to blame.

The next session I went to was a one to one with a slightly overweight woman called Maria. Because my time at The Abbey was relatively short, she had looked at my notes and told the staff that she had to have a session with me. I walked up the grand oak staircase to her office on the first floor. It was lucky that this journey took place near the end of my treatment as I definitely wouldn't have been able to manage the grand oak staircase on my first few days. She took me into her office and sat down with me, her eyes smiling at me, her voice kind. I felt comfortable around this woman, I trusted her. It was the first time I'd trusted any of the staff members there. Maria asked me a few questions about how I felt about my body, how I felt about myself as a person. I repeated the same answer that I always did when faced with this question;

"I don't really like my body, but its ok I guess. I'm alright, I think that I'm a good friend".

Her eyes looked at my face as I spoke and then found my own and gazed into them so piercingly that it shocked me slightly, as though there was a surge of current as she stared me down,

"You're lying."

"No I'm not" I insisted. My acting skill had always managed to convince anyone that worked on me on a therapist/patient level, but this woman seemed to be the exception. She was the kryptonite to my Superman.

"Tell me the truth Emily, I'm not interested in what you think I want to hear, I want to know what you think".

I sat there thinking; bugger now this woman is going to think I am crazy, self-obsessed, vain, shallow or just a downright horrible person. I took a breath,

"I hate my body. I hate it. I hate the way it feels, I hate the way it moves, I hate the way it functions. I don't want people to look at it, I like it slightly better than my face but only because I know I can change it. I'm fat but I can get thin. I'm stuck with my face unfortunately, if I could change that I would. Every time I see my reflection I'm repulsed. Every time I put something into my body I feel sick because it doesn't deserve food, it's too big as it is. I'd rather be a thin corpse than live a long fat life…..and because I think like this I must be a horrible person. I'm so selfish and self-obsessed I must be disgusting on the inside as well as on the outside. I can pretend that I am happy and bubbly for a bit, I do pretend for the people around me but it takes so much out of me. I've been acting for years….basically, I hate my body and I hate myself, if I could switch with one person even if it was just for a day I would jump at the chance".

I finished my rant and Maria sat for a minute, looking at me and taking it all in. The minute I stopped I felt ashamed, so I decided to count the flecks in the carpet to distract myself from her stare.

"Get up" Maria said, standing up and motioning for me to follow.

I was petrified she was going to throw me out of the office for being so silly; march me out of The Priory doors "You're not ill, you're just a wallowing idiot" but instead she started to lay out large pieces of paper and taped them together so the floor became a huge canvas. She asked me to take my layers off so I was left in underwear and lie down. Then she marked various different points around my body, and she handed me the pen.

"Draw on this piece of paper what your body looks like when you are lying down, so when you are at your largest point, make sure you keep it life-size and in proportion".

I stared at the paper, pulled the cap off the pen, (which even then took some effort as I was about as strong as a kitten) knelt down and started to draw. With each line I felt like I wanted to cry more, this looked so disgusting already. I was naturally so out of proportion and so short that I couldn't stand what I was creating. I stood up when it was finished and then just broke down. There it was, the reality of it -so ugly, so lumpy and so big. Maria gave me a hug and told me to man up, which made me giggle slightly. We'd only met today but she seemed to already know my humour.

The next thing I had to do was lie down again on the drawing of myself I'd completed and let Maria draw around my body. I was certain I hadn't drawn my outline big enough so I was mentally preparing to see her lines overlapping mine.

I stood up and stared down. I couldn't take it in. I didn't believe it.

Right in front of me were two outlines of a body. My body and the outline that was smaller was drawn in Maria's pen. How? The difference was shocking; my body was about half the size of what I thought. It felt like somebody had knocked down a wall in front of me and for the first time I saw what everyone else saw. I was thin but I had curves, the belly that I hated for years didn't look so big when you looked at it as part of the rest of my body. My legs weren't stumps and my wrists were tiny. Who the hell had replaced all the mirrors in my world with circus trick ones?

I was forced to face the reality that I really truly had body dysmorphia, that my view of myself was so distorted and so wrong. But if my eyes had seen something completely different to reality, did that mean that I had been punishing myself and hating my body for most of my life for nothing? Why? Why had I done this to myself?

I left the session, canvas folded up in hand, shaking. I felt confused and lost. I didn't know what was right or wrong anymore. It took me a long time to take that information in and at times I had to look at that drawing again because my brain kept convincing itself that it was a fluke or it was a lie. I owe a lot to Maria. Without her I would have never realised just how dysfunctional my brain could be and how futile any attempts to starve myself or purge were. After all, if all you see in the mirror is ugliness and negativity that's not your true reflection, that's the reflection in your head and that will never change unless you start to CHOOSE to see yourself differently.

Find the goodness and beauty in yourself. You'll save yourself a lot of heartache.

Fifteen

2012

A diary entry written a few weeks before my admission into The Abbey:

"I sat at my sisters, on the stairs while everyone else was outside, watching the fireworks and kind of wishing I was one of them. The ability to burst into something grand and beautiful and then cease to exist. No feeling, no sense of time, just a moment of pure unbridled colour and then nothingness.

Sometimes I think I drive to crash…It sounds crazy and stupid I know, but it's like a test to see if I should really be here…walking around and "living"…I caught myself today daring to pull out in front of a speeding lorry and then remembered that someone else would be driving it. I couldn't kill someone else, that wouldn't be fair. Afterwards I found myself driving that little bit too close to the side of the road, turning that little bit too slow and driving way too fast. Or I'd feel the impulse to just swerve off the road and see what happens. I'm not saying that I ever will necessarily crash on purpose. I know how stupid that would be, as usual my head keeps a mildly sensible hold on reality. Some days though, it's just so tempting…"

The next morning I was woken by the man upstairs in the dementia ward slamming his fists against the walls and screaming "BANG, BANG,

BANG". His episodes like this could last for half an hour and the first time I heard him I was petrified. It felt as though I was in an insane asylum; sex addict to the left of me, crazy man above. After a while though I became used to this man's screaming and banging about and decided to call him George. George liked to make a lot of noise, just the same way that Marc liked to sniff a lot of coke and I liked to make myself throw up a lot. We were all part of the same gig here and there's no use being afraid of something that can't hurt you. So that was George, my morning alarm.

The day began with a typical breakfast of 2 slices of toast with jam, bran flakes, semi skimmed milk and a piece of fruit. I think most of the patients on the ED ward could spread that one meal out into 4 days and by this point I certainly wanted to. After breakfast I rolled back down to the ward, fused myself onto the sofa....there may as well have been an Emily-sized impression on the cushions from the amount of time I had to spend there. Thoughts of yesterday were still racing around in my head. How had I developed such a mistaken view of my body? I knew that if you stared at a particular part of your body in the mirror it appears bigger than it usually is. I knew that everyone sees themselves in a slightly different, more critical way than others do, but I had nearly killed myself in the process of getting thinner on the basis of a lie. It didn't take away how I felt though. This frustrated me; I still felt horrible and ugly and fat, I was still uncomfortable in my own skin. How could I still feel so grotesque after I had been proven wrong, after I had seen the truth with my own eyes? I was taken out of my thoughts by one of the staff members, Sue, walking in and beckoning me to talk to her. She was my point of contact during my stay and the person I was meant to talk to about how I was feeling and managing in the Abbey, but I never did because I didn't like her much; she was the one that kept warning me away from Marc. She led me to a little office and sat me down.

"First of all" Sue trawled in her overly well-spoken voice "We need to talk about Marc. Despite me telling you that patient relationships aren't allowed here you've continued to talk to him and we've decided that you aren't allowed in the Addiction Treatment Patients' lounge anymore and we're doing it for your wellbeing as well as Marc's."

I was immediately annoyed. Nothing had

even happened and now I was being banned from a communal area like a child. I said nothing, nodded and looked down at the floor.

"Secondly we've decided we want you to stay a little longer, if you're here for the weekend then you can go straight back into day treatment at Browns on Monday so there isn't a period of time where you feel left alone, so you can manage the transition better."

I could do nothing but stare at her.

"So if you don't have anything to say to me then I'll let you get on, we've put you into a body image group so you'd better make your way there."

I stood up, thanked her and left to go to group. Walking up the corridor, I felt like the walls were closing in around me.

I was scared, I didn't want to stay longer. I was fed up of being treated with zero trust, fed up of being watched all the time, fed up of not even being able to use the loo without someone there. I was so angry at everyone around me, but I knew that if I blew up and told people how I really felt and reacted in a way I wanted to, I'd be classed as unstable and they'd probably just keep me there longer. Bastards. I hated this place.

As usual I bottled it up and walked into group as calmly as I could. The session did not go well; we had to focus on a part of our body that we didn't like and think about what we tell ourselves about it. I couldn't think which part I hated the most. I couldn't find one positive part despite the good that I had discovered the day before. I didn't want to talk about it. I couldn't cope with it. I wanted to rip my skin off and pull out the fat underneath. It would probably kill me but at least it would be gone and I wouldn't feel this way anymore. This was too much and I couldn't hold back my tears. I got up and walked out, not even excusing myself. I got back to the ward with tears flowing freely down my face and saw Jeff - the guy that had caught me in Marc's room - who immediately motioned me out of the ward and took me for a cigarette. He was one of the staff that wasn't so uptight; he spoke like an aged hippy and was covered in tattoos that he had either done himself or had done in his younger years when he had been put in a cell more than once. Jeff didn't give you any bullshit and would give it to you straight. His life experience was so broad and messed up and integral to what made him an amazing staff member. He helped me so much during my time at The Abbey.

"You need to let it out man" he said helping me light my second cigarette

"You just take all this emotion out on yourself all the time because you don't want to hurt anyone else, but that's not cool man cuz after a while you're just destroying yourself".

I told him all the reasons I was angry, knowing he wouldn't judge me and he told me that I needed to see Sue again but this time actually talk to her - shout at her, swear at her if I needed to - anything was better than taking it out on myself and bottling it all up.

"That or get some wacky baccy maann and chill out".

Jeff always knew how to make me feel better and his jokes referring to his past made me feel like he was a real person, not that the other staff members were robots, but he had a coloured past and wasn't afraid to share it with you. This made you appreciate his advice so much more because it was honest. I knew I had to stand my ground in the impending ward round which would decide how my treatment would continue. I stubbed out the cigarette, walked back to the lounge, put my headphones in and turned my music on then cried until I slept.

Later on I felt a little better. I'd let everything out in the open and the sleep had done me wonders. After lunch and dinner had been eaten: full portions, pudding included, hated every second, I counted down the minutes till I was freed from the ED lounge. I immediately went outside to smoke and met Marc. We talked about our days and about our opinions of the staff and then decided that if I wasn't allowed in the ATP lounge we'd sit in the hallway and chat. The staff would be able to see us from reception so why would it be a problem? After 5 minutes, Hope, one of the night nurses, came over to us and told us to move. She was a big African woman who wore fabulous head scarves and terrified the life out of me. We asked her if we could go into the lounge, to which she pointed out I wasn't allowed in there so we said we'd stay in the hallway then because we wanted to talk. She walked off and started muttering to the staff on reception. We decided to go for another cigarette so they'd chill out about us being in the hallway and as we walked by the desk everything just kicked off.

"There's obviously something more than friendship going on here" Hope boomed.

"You can't get too close to each other you're bad news"

I was seething. I was unbelievably fed up of being watched and being judged - all for being friends with someone that was attractive. Despite the room incident, Marc and I hadn't done anything wrong. We both fought our corner and stood up for ourselves and our friendship. After shutting Hope up we walked outside. I was sick of it and sick of them.

There we go Jeff, I definitely didn't bottle that one in! We sat in the cold November air smoking and trying to calm down. This was ridiculous, all the fuss over nothing, it was just getting out of hand.

We agreed to just text each other and not see each other in the evenings to pacify the staff. There was nothing they could do about us texting each other…although they would probably try.

I walked back in and saw Bella, who I'd sat with the night Marc relapsed, and with one look we decided to go back to my room so I could tell her everything that had just happened. We sat ranting about the staff and then before I could prepare myself she started talking about her abuse as a child. It was horrible to think that someone could do that to another person, it was worse to know that it was her brother, but the sad reality is that is the world we live in. People are cruel. As we sat talking, Marc walked up the corridor and stood outside the bedroom door. There were three of us, he wasn't in my room. I mean, what was going to happen, some kind of weird orgy?! Hope walked past, stopped

"You two are addicted to each other!" she

walked off, exasperated.

We all just looked at each other and started laughing; not only had Bella not been told off for being in another patients room, which is apparently strictly forbidden, but Hope had used the word 'addicted'. Brilliant choice seeing as we were all some kind of addiction patients. It was ridiculous. I left to go smoke on my own, proving that I was capable of breaking this "addiction to Marc" and go solo and on my way back he and I bumped into each other, exchanging a quick, strictly banned hug. Wow, breaking the rules felt so fun.

Later that evening I sat in my room watching Bridget Jones again. There was a knock on the door and Marc came in to crash a roll up. The door shut and I felt a surge of electricity which made me sit up straight. We were alone. No one could see us. The crescendo of the evening had led up to this moment. What I wouldn't give to look up and kiss him, run my hands through his hair and be held in his muscular arms. He was so beautiful. But like a wave, the moment passed. The thought had crashed over me, causing my heart to beat faster, my body to tingle and then it left. I gave him the cigarette and a quick hug and he was gone. Damn.

Sixteen

The next morning I woke up early as usual after hourly night sweats, decided to have a cigarette and then sit in the lounge going through my 'learning portfolio'. I opened the folder and turned to the page I had filled in the day before:

Section 10: MYSELF

1- What am I like?   *"Honest, loyal, reasonable, patient."*

2- What do I like most about me?   *"I give people the benefit of that doubt, try not to be judgemental, I'd like to think I'm caring…"*

3- What do I dislike most about me?   *"My appearance, my inability to keep a relationship, my negativity, my lack of self-worth."*

4- How do other people see me?

And there was Marc's handwriting, answering the fourth question…

"Fun, caring, intelligent, pretty, giving, thoughtful, understanding."

then Bella's:

"Artistic, funny, friendly, loving, caring, selfless, puts other people first, compassionate, pretty, clever."

Two people I had only just met really, two people that saw so much more in me than I did. Was I wrong? Or were they?

I flicked to the next section:

"What Am I Afraid Of?

1   What are the most frightening things to me?   *"I'm frightened of failing, falling, being alone, not being able to cope, my family or friends dying and leaving me".*

2   When was I aware of being afraid of these things?   *"About a year ago. When I lost Nanny......it felt as though my heart broke apart and I still don't feel whole."*

3   What has made me afraid of these things?   *"When Nanny died and I realised I'd never be in her arms again. The fact that I dwell on my failures, I feel like a failure and that I am good at nothing, I am so rubbish at relationships I feel lonely a lot of the time. Having to leave my uni course because I collapsed and having to defer drama school in London makes me worried I may never be able to get there and keep going."*

So many questions that I had to answer and

all it did was give me a headache and hate my life even more. I threw the sheets on the floor and started to draw. After breakfast, I had a 'food and mood' group which I spent half asleep and then I killed time until lunch trying to forget my impending ward round. I was dreading it; a meeting with all the important members of staff and the dietician to talk about my treatment and supervision. I knew they'd bring up Marc and I'd be in the shit for what had happened the previous night. My Doctor came and found me and took me up to the room. I opened the door and everyone's eyes were upon me, looking me up and down as though trying to work out whether I had been cured yet. I sat there as they discussed me, waiting for the Marc talk but thankfully it never came. Instead I was granted 'zero supervision'; my bathroom would be unlocked, I could go to dinner and eat with the ATP patients, I didn't have to stay in that one god forsaken room every single hour of every single day. I was elated. I felt almost free. That evening I ate with some of the ATP patients, I laughed and for the first time I wasn't concentrating on the food in front of me. I was enjoying myself.

For the next few days I felt a lot better about my environment. There were a few dark moments when my reflux tried to get the better of me. I had to fight to keep food down. I was tempted to use my newly unlocked bathroom to throw up but something in me stopped it from happening. I had the opportunity to stop my illness, to try and leave it behind me and the voice in my head told me if I didn't try as hard as I could now I may never stop. I'd die of it or live the rest of my life clouded in an eating disorder. Why would I want that? After so much hard work? It was time to fight.

My last morning greeted me with pink skies and frost. The first of December had arrived. I watched the sky change from pink to a cool blue, the ground and bushes around me were enveloped in white frost. It was beautiful. I spent a lot of my time during my last few days playing cards with the boys and laughing about nothing, proper belly laughs that I had forgotten about for so long, shaking your body and warming you to the tips of your fingers. Marc and I now had free reign of the place and no one could tell us off. Sure, the staff carried on trying to separate us but we weren't breaking the rules, so instead the staff descended into a stony silence. We'd spent the evening before watching films in the lounge with a blanket over us. I'd feel a surge of current every time our hands brushed or our bodies got a bit too close. We spoke about my return into day treatment which I was dreading with every single fibre of my body. I was managing here finally and I felt like it would be ruined with the change in treatment. I wasn't sure that I was ready to step down. There was nothing I could do though. My body may have been recovering but my mind wasn't; it was still cankered with thoughts that shouldn't belong there.

When the evening was turning to morning we decided to go to bed. He walked me back up the corridor to my room to say goodnight. It was the last time that he would. As he looked into my eyes I felt that same rush that I'd experienced when we were accidentally alone. I wanted him to hold me and never let me go, put his hands through my hair and kiss me. He smiled as if he knew what I was thinking and turned to walk away. Before I knew it, I had grabbed his hand and pulled him into me, our lips locking, my heart racing, our bodies meeting finally after so long. I was in ecstasy, I felt alive. We pulled apart. I half expected Hope to be behind us ready to kill, but we were still alone. In one hedonistic moment I had not only completely broken the rules, but lost myself entirely. I hadn't felt this happy in years. I went to bed that night with the biggest grin on my face and it hadn't disappeared.

"I believe in pink. I believe that laughing is the best calorie burner. I believe in kissing, kissing a lot. I believe in being strong when everything seems to be going wrong. I believe that happy girls are the prettiest girls. I believe that tomorrow is another day and I believe in miracles." |
Audrey Hepburn

I smiled at the morning, my last morning, and the last time I would sit in this chair smoking and wishing to be home. In a matter of hours, I would be free. I would be free and the world was beautiful

Seventeen

"Take a step back. Look at yourself. You are human; you are beautiful and you can be anything. You can be everything. Do not hate everyone because someone broke your heart, or because your parents split up, or the kid down the street called you fat, ugly, worthless. Do not concern yourself with things that you cannot control. Cry when you need to and let go when it's time. Don't hang onto painful memories just because you're afraid to forget.

Stop taking things for granted.

Live for something, live for yourself.

Fall in love, fall out of love, fall in love, fall out of love, do this over and over until you know what real love truly is. Question things; tell people how you really feel.

Sleep under the stars. Create. Imagine. Inspire. Share something wonderful. Meet new people. Make someone's day. Follow your dreams. Live your life to its full potential.

Just live dammit.

Let go of all the horrible things in your life and just drop everything and live."

- Kendall Fithian

Eighteen

2012

Breathe. Just breathe. My whole body was shaking and my eyes were sore. I had been crying the whole night. The day I had been dreading for all the time I was in The Abbey had arrived. As I walked through the security doors and into the day treatment area, the familiar smell greeted me; cooking food. It was taking me all I had not to panic and run back out.

I had been in day treatment before. In my second year at university I was cast in the end of year musical. During rehearsals one day in March 2012 I started to feel dizzy and sick. I stood up to go through a scene and the room started to blur, it was boiling, why had no one opened a window? How was no one else sweating like I was? I felt sick, I had to be sick. I ran blindly to the toilet across the corridor and collapsed into the toilet bowl heaving up nothing (I didn't keep anything I ate down) sweating, retching, shaking. My friend came in, I hadn't closed the cubicle door. I couldn't see, I couldn't breathe. I felt her hand on my back rubbing me, my other friend was there too, her hands pulling my hair back away from my face. I crawled into the corner of the bathroom, heaving, hyperventilating. I was going to die. I was sure of it. This was it.

My vision blurred again, the uni first aider was called, she spent ages trying to get me to breathe normally but why should I breathe when it was my time to die? I was ready to die. I wanted to die. Every single day when I drove to uni I'd dare myself to crash, to career off the road and over the edge and plunge myself into the darkness. I didn't want to be alive anymore. For privacy while the paramedics arrived, I was taken into my tutor's office and sat down, all the time trying to concentrate on returning my breathing to normal. I was sick again, this time in their bin, yellow bile filled my mouth and cascaded into the bin below. After what seemed like hours my breathing calmed and my vision came back. The paramedics sat with me, asking me questions. For the first time in my life, I admitted I was bulimic in front of people I knew. Two of my best friends and my tutors now knew my secret. My lies were split apart and I had to suffer the consequences. I was admitted into day treatment, left university and the course I had spent my whole life trying to succeed in.

The first time at day treatment did nothing for me. I met some amazing people, namely Millie; a gorgeous and unbelievably clever girl only a year younger than me who had battled with anorexia ever since she was 12, who would become one of my closest friends. There was also Heather; nearly 10 years older than me but thought the same as I did and had the ability to make anyone fall in love with her, I certainly did. Those girls kept me above water during the first round of treatment; they kept me smiling and reminded me how to laugh. But there were a lot more problems I had to face; eating huge portions that I wasn't physically or mentally ready for, talking about my weight and causing it to become a main feature in my life and how I thought about myself, eating three meals and three snacks and having to keep it down- something I'd never done before. But one of the worst parts was Jackie; an anorexic that had been ill for so long that she was toxic. Every single problem that someone had she'd had but worse. Day treatment became the 'Jackie show' and because of the things that she said I started to feel inadequate, like I wasn't ill enough, like I wasn't strong enough to be an anorexic, so I wasn't good enough to be in treatment. We had to weigh ourselves once a week and every week she got lower and I got higher... I was the fat one of the group, the outcast. Jackie never meant to make me feel that way but I let her. In reality she had no one. No friends, no family like mine, anorexia was all she had and she tried to lie her way out by attaching weights to herself on weigh days, walking incessantly and not eating at home but lying to say that she had. She was ill, I was ill, we were in the same boat, but I just couldn't see it. After a few months at day treatment I started lying and being sick more than ever. All my intake sheets were filled with made up meals and snacks and I'd binge as often as I could at home, running for miles, starving myself. I was a mess. The only thing I had taken from my first round of day treatment was a newfound obsession with weighing myself, because weight mattered, weight told me whether I was getting too fat or had eaten too much that day. I never wanted to go back, I never thought I'd have to, but here I was. A day patient once more.

This time around however, I promised myself no more lies, no more pretending I was coping when I couldn't. For my second stint, I knew that the only way to get better was to be honest even if it was the hardest thing in the world. I'd come too far to go back. I walked into the familiar room in day treatment and sitting on one of the ridiculously uncomfortable blue chairs was Millie. Her smile lit up the room and her presence immediately made me ten times stronger. I was back with someone who knew me, someone who understood me, someone I could trust to never judge but always be honest with me. I could do it this time around. I had to.

Nineteen

The first few days back at Day Treatment were hard, really hard. My first day consisted of the usual introductions; "I'm Emily, I've had an eating disorder for seven years, just come out of The Abbey, know a few of you already....I don't really know what else to say..."

My only shining lights were the girls I had met during my first stint, Millie and Heather. Seeing them made me feel safer and, despite every bone in my body screaming to get out, I managed to smile and get on with it, or at least try to. There is an atmosphere of sadness in treatment, one that I had managed to escape in hospital because Marc could take my mind away from it. Here though, it was impossible. They cover over the mirrors, as though trying to stop the patients from seeing the sadness and pain in their eyes. Being in a room of beautiful people, strong people, brave people, but all completely broken is difficult, because no one can see what they are really worth. I'd known Millie for a while now and I'd seen how hard she appeared to fight but when I really looked at her sometimes it felt as though she had already given up. It killed me. I wanted her to see her kindness, her beauty, her wit and her cleverness but she was blind to it, blinkered by anorexia. I'd never hated it as much until I realised what it had done to her. My beautiful broken friend. I'd have done anything to save her.

There were three constant staff members in Browns day treatment center; Clive, Norah and Chloe. Clive and Norah were older and although they had a wealth of experience, I was always on edge around them. Clive listened but never seemed to understand. I didn't want to tell him anything because it felt like there was a personality clash. I didn't trust him. Norah was Welsh, bubbly and creative, she acted like a mother hen to the group and her activities with us were always art based and it enabled us to have an hour or so not thinking about our weight or about food but just to have fun; whether it be painting cups or making cards, it was a breath of fresh air. It made us feel slightly more normal. Chloe was closer in age to me and she helped to connect the staff to the patients. Despite not being a part of the mental health services for as long as the others, she was so valuable because it felt like she was always really listening to everything that you had to say, always learning and never stereotyping you into a box of patients that she had encountered before. I think some forget that when they work with people all the time, they forget that each individual has a life and different triggers, different pain. Human beings are so complex that no matter whether you have the same illness as someone else, your reasoning for it isn't the same. The way you think about it isn't the same and the way you cope with it isn't the same. That's why some people can live with depression for years and others commit suicide. Try as our society may, we can never be put into boxes. We aren't statistics; we are humans, and most of the time that's all we ever ask to be treated like.

The first few days I hardly spoke to the staff, or anyone for that matter, save Heather and Millie. I didn't want to share, I didn't want to talk about how I felt. The first time I was there I thought it would be the cure and it wasn't, I had lost faith. I wasn't sure if it could help me now. I struggled with the food - portion sizes were huge in comparison to the Abbey and my reflux went into overdrive. I couldn't have a proper conversation with anyone because sick would constantly flow in and out of my mouth, I'd hide my face so people couldn't see how revolting my constant swallowing was, so they couldn't see how disgusting and greedy and fat I was. I was so embarrassed. Gaviscon didn't help, tablets didn't help. It wouldn't have even mattered if I ate small portions; I was never free from it. I'd lie in bed at night still suffering and for the first few nights I cried myself to sleep. It was hard enough forcing myself to eat, it was near impossible when I was constantly regurgitating. I immediately started cutting out my snacks that I was meant to eat at home, I couldn't bring myself to force more fat into my body. I was a stone heavier, that was more than enough for me and my body obviously didn't want it because it wouldn't keep fighting back. There was no escape in the hours I was at day treatment however; mammoth portions, weigh days and talking about how we felt in a group scenario. This was my reality and I had to just get on with it. My logical brain knew this, but I felt like I was just fighting a losing battle.

Living back at home with my mother and stepdad was also taking its toll. They lived in the middle of nowhere so I would drive an hour to get to treatment and then have to come back in the evening. I hated being somewhere so remote, but why? It's not like I had any friends that were desperate to see me in Cheltenham. I'd managed to push most of them away and I was mostly alone. I'd spend all the time that I wasn't at

Browns in bed; curled up, warm and protected. Completely ignoring the real world and life outside of my room. I had no desire to be part of it. What was the point?

After the first day back, I came home and found that my mirror in my room had been replaced. I was mortified. When I moved to London I had got it cheap from the shop down the road and it was only a little while later that I realised that it was one of those wonderful mirrors that made you look thin. Perfect! I no longer had to feel repulsed when I looked in the mirror because I could see a thinner version of myself. But mum had replaced it. She said it was bad for me to look at, that it made people look horrible and too thin. It's like she wanted me to see how fat I was. Why would she want to do that to me? I looked in the glass and was horrified. Staring back at me through the mirror was the thirteen year old girl crying in the toilets at the school disco. I felt the same hate towards myself that I had discovered that night. I was so disgusting and I was huge. It tore me apart; I couldn't look at myself any longer.

The next day I walked into day treatment with that image in my head. I wanted to throw

every single piece of food they put in front of me
at the wall, smash the plates, refuse to eat, but I
knew I couldn't. It wouldn't be fair for everyone
else who was probably thinking similar things sat
around the tables. So I stayed silent. I kept going
through the motions and not really investing
myself. After a day spent mainly locked in my
own thoughts, I started the journey back to Mums
in the forest. I was so full, it hurt, but I was
peckish. How was that possible? I had taken a
snack with me to eat....one that I hadn't planned
on eating. I was meant to but I didn't want to. It
was my 'challenge': chocolate. Driving along the
motorway I opened the wrapper and placed a
piece into my mouth and sucked. It tasted good. I
hadn't allowed myself chocolate for years. I
decided, when I was 17, my New Years
Resolution was that I wouldn't eat chocolate for a
whole year. That year had turned into two, three,
then four. I had another piece, and then another,
I finished the whole of the snack sized bar by the
time I was out in the sticks. I enjoyed it, it was
delicious.

    Suddenly a wave of guilt crashed into
me,stopping me in my tracks and a voice in my
head started screaming:

"You absolute fat idiot, what have you done? Do you realise how much you have eaten fatty? Does your little stupid fat brain really think that your disgusting fat body needs chocolate? You don't need it, you don't deserve it, you're so unbelievably pathetic and you can't even control what you eat. You're not good enough. Fat, pathetic, ugly."

So much noise in my head, each word like a physical blow, so much pain and torment, it was horrible. I wanted to scream back but I was in so much of a panic I stopped paying attention to where I was or what I was doing. I pulled over somewhere in the woods, opened my car door and threw up everywhere. Everything I had eaten that day falling onto the floor. My reflux was having a party, it didn't have to fight anymore, and it didn't need to keep working so hard to keep food in because now I was letting it out.

All the anger and sadness and embarrassment that I had felt over the last few weeks was all coming out. For the first time in seventeen days I was sick. I hadn't lasted that long in seven years.

Afterwards I sat in my car for a while, exhausted, crying and hitting my head on the steering wheel. I felt my disappointment as though it were physical pain. Thoughts tormenting me still. What had I done?

Twenty

2012

"*Sometimes I think that I'm crazy.*

I feel crazy.

I have two sides to my brain, just like everyone else; the logical and illogical (emotion fueled). But I don't seem to cope with it as well as everyone else. I don't know why. I could be a therapist's field day.

My logical brain is switched on most of the time, I know why I feel certain things, I know why I do certain things and what I should and shouldn't do. How I should and shouldn't act. It recognises when I am thinking as Emily or as ill Emily, it distinguishes, it reasons, it understands. But my logical brain is constantly under pressure; sometimes I can almost feel it. I feel the battle.

There's an ongoing war against the illogical, ill side of me. It's as though I've managed to cover the wrong side of my brain over with a sheet and every now and then it fights back, punctures a hole and bursts through. When I'm sick, when I binge and often when I'm alone, my illogical side overthrows my reasoning and sense and I am powerless to resist, I don't want to struggle against it, I embrace the madness and let it wash all over me. Because maybe I am mad? Because maybe then when it's over, I'll appreciate how great normal life can be?

At times I feel like I have to let my crazy side out just to be able to function and cope. Other times I run scenarios through my head; threatening my family and loved ones with words or knives, forcing them not to care about me so they can let me die in peace. Doing something unstable around people so I'll be taken away. I once used to think about sitting in the garden while everyone was out and slashing my wrists and letting the blood colour the grass red or jumping from the balcony and letting my crumpled body lie there until it gave out. I fantasize about these moments, or rather my bad brain does.

Every time I've tried to commit suicide or had the urge to go mad at someone my good brain would kick in and reason, whether it be before I started cutting/drinking/ pill popping or when I was halfway through, it would always intervene before it was too late. My good brain always saves my life. My good brain knew that I was too logical to finish myself off.

At points I hate my mind. Sometimes I want to just let go of my reasoning, my sense, my sanity and just give in to madness and forget myself and who I was. I am on a precipice and eager to dive off. I want to be anything besides myself, anything as long as I had no memory of what I was before. If I was mad and always had been mad in memory then there was nothing left to lose. But I can't, life doesn't work that way.

I am a fighter; I will always be a fighter, I have no choice in that.. I wish that I could melt my bad brain away and be left with clarity and balance but there will always be a bad brain and a good brain. Sometimes it makes me cry, other times it makes me feel stronger. I will always be in a battle. I am Emily. This is me. Some things in life you have to accept and carry with you, maybe this was my baggage? Maybe this is the thing that makes me human?"

2018

When I was going through the motions of treatment I often felt like there were two sides to me; one that wanted to get better and on that felt safe in the illness. I identified them as separate entities and often spoke about the battle inside myself - believing that this was what my life would always be like.

It wasn't until a long while later that I realised that we are the only ones who have the power to take control of our lives. I was unknowingly choosing to create a battle within myself between good and evil and instead of truly opening myself up to light and love, I had the door half open which was causing me to be imbalanced and torn between two paths.

The writer Eckhart Tolle once identified that at the beginning of his period of self-discovery he felt sick of himself. This led him to start to see his behaviours and negative thoughts and feelings as belonging to a separate part of himself. Once he realised this, he made the conscious decision to let it go and move forward with lightness and new found freedom. He realised that he didn't *have* to carry what no longer served him and was able to leave it all behind. I had the power to do the same - I just had to believe it.

It knew in my heart that I had more to do, more to give and so much to live for but I also told myself that I was weak, I was ill, I was broken. I believed that in order to get better I had to fight and battle against myself, when in reality the opposite was the case. Instead of holding onto limiting beliefs, rules and habits I needed to trust myself and my body and believe that I had the power to create long lasting positive change without having to struggle. It was possible but I still had some lessons to learn before I truly believed it.

Twenty One

2012

The day after I broke my winning streak I hardly spoke. I had so much to think about and so much to process. I had previously told myself that if The Abbey didn't work then I would have to commit myself to a life with an eating disorder, I didn't believe anything else would work, but now it had happened I wasn't sure that I could. I knew for a fact that it would get bad, if I entered into being ill again there may be no way out. I could die. I was confused; I wasn't sure if I wanted to live or die. I carried on with the structure that I had planned out for me; Day Treatment. It was the few hours in the day I felt safe from myself, if not restricted. I just had to keep going through the motions until it started to work.

As Marc and I continued to text and he continued to brighten up my days, I started thinking about Sam; I'd spent years of my life chasing after the wrong boy; someone that had made me feel so inescapably inadequate, someone who had hardly bothered to see how I was despite knowing I was in The Abbey. Sam was only there when he wanted to be and didn't seem to care when I needed him. Our time in Australia felt like forever ago. I decided it was time to say goodbye for good, it was time I deserved better. That evening I sent a message which I never thought I could.

"Hey...

So really I don't know where to begin...I've just been staring at a blank screen for ages.

I want to get this out because for so many years every time you broke my heart I've just kept it bottled up, because I've always believed that you and I still have a chance, even when you've hurt me again and again, I was worried that if I really told you how I felt, or got angry with you that you would leave me forever, and even now that thought scares me.

For the past 6 years you have come in and out of my life so sporadically, it's like you have an internal sensor that when I meet someone new that I consider having a relationship with bang, there you are again, reminding me how I once felt. Or when I finally start to believe that I can get along just fine without you, you reappear and make me remember how happy I am when I am with you. It's my own fault really because I never learn, and most recently when you reappeared, instead of protecting myself and not seeing you I was worried about you and wanted to make sure you were okay. So I said yes to meeting up, and once again was reminded just how great things are when we are together in each other's company. That's the thing, I always put you first over me, and yes, again, it probably is my fault for being so stupid and believing that things will be different over and over again but I can't believe that you would be so heartless to keep doing that to me. But I keep being proven wrong, because you always leave. In the past you've led me to believe that you loved me, led me to believe that we'd be together, given me some "future" to look forward to and then turned around and been with another girl. The last time, right in front of my face. And still, I forgave you.

I used to write diaries and kept them all from when I was little. From the first time I met you to our time together recently I had it all documented, every single happy moment; from our talks in the graveyard, our first kiss, all those days spent in bed watching TV, playing the wii with your sisters, when you picked me up and span me round and kissed me, New Year's Eve, kissing in the rain in Australia, lying next to each other for hours. All the promises we made, the way you smiled at me and called me beautiful, the way I feel when I'm with you; like everything is good. I've destroyed them all now but it hasn't erased them from my memories. But what I had forgotten was every time you let me down, every time I was told not to trust you, to stay away, that you were texting other girls, that you were sleeping with other girls, all the times that you suddenly out of the blue had a girlfriend that you would then stay with but then still manage to make me believe you had feelings for me, the death threats I got from Georgia and eventual fights I got into with her…fights that I never once fought back in because I didn't want to upset anyone. I cried over and over again, I've questioned for years why I'm not good enough for you, why it always is "not the right time right now"…is that really it? Or is it simply that you just don't like me that much, and if it is, why do you keep coming back and reliving the past? Making me relive it. Is it curiosity? Is it love? Or is it simply that I'm the go to girl that you always know is stupid enough to be there?

I know it's not all your fault, and again I feel like I don't want to blame you in case I lose you but I just don't think you get it. I have had 6 years with an eating disorder. I tracked it back in my diaries and although before I met you I had extreme body issues, was bullied horrifically and hated the way I looked, after the first time you ended things, I spiralled. You confirmed to me albeit unknowingly, that I wasn't good enough, the evil disorder in my mind latched onto the fact that I couldn't keep the boy I thought I was in love with. I concluded that I was too fat, too ugly, not good enough, not confident enough, not sexual enough and for the next few years I hid behind so many masks that I've come out of it not entirely sure who I really am. I lost weight, and at certain points every year you would come back to me and I started to think in those moments that what I was doing to myself was the right way to go to get you back, that "no one loves a fatty" and that by being thin I would finally look good enough for you. Of course, my eating disorder started to branch out and away from just that. My life is entirely intertwined in it now, it's my comfort, a way to destroy myself, a way to congratulate myself, the way I feel better, the way I punish myself, the way to run from life…it is one big fucked up mess that circles back into not being good enough. That is simply what I am. I destroy the life around me and destroy myself simultaneously because I don't feel I deserve happiness.

So no, I'm not blaming you for the mess that I have got myself into because it's really not your fault, but the fact that you don't even know this has been going on with me for the past 6 years. Why doesn't that tell me that really, you just don't care enough? You've never realised how sad I've been. Since my Nan died in 2011 I have fallen into a horrible hole of depression which has again mixed in with my eating disorder, making it all the more difficult to recover from. It felt like my world fell apart. A part of me died as I sat there with her body. Things went from bad to worse. I collapsed in rehearsals. I had to go into a day clinic and give up university so that I can try to learn to eat properly again. I have had counselling weekly. I am on drugs just to keep me alive. I could technically have a heart attack at any given moment because my potassium is so low. I was told I'd be dead by the end of 2012 if I didn't change things. I tried to kill myself....at times I still want to kill myself. You don't know any of this. You never have asked. It's always me saying "how are you?" "Tell me the truth, is everything okay". I genuinely worry about how you feel and how you are doing, even when it's about the fact that you have just broken up with a girl you love. It kills me sometimes that I'm not that girl, but I'll still be there to pick up the pieces because I never want to think of you alone and crying. I've tried to hate you because you've hurt me, but even then I would never have wished that on you.

I need to open my eyes and realise that your promises to me are empty. That you've just kept me on a lead, that you yank back every now and again just to remind me that I think I'm in love with you. I still blame myself, I still think that I'm just not good enough for you even when my friends say I don't deserve to be treated the way that you've treated me. Anyone else and I would have been rid of them. I don't let myself get pushed around by anyone else, hell; I've never cared that much about anyone else. I don't let people in. But you, you're like my kryptonite.

I would love to believe that we are meant for each other like you say we are. More than anything I would want for us to be married and stable, with the jobs and the life that you say that we'll have. But I need to stop believing it, because all you've ever proved is that you'll leave me again. You'll leave me questioning myself, what I've done wrong and missing you every hour of every day. Do I deserve it?

Please stop lying to me. Please don't come back into my life if you aren't going to stay. I need you to respect me enough to realise that what you do to me, maybe without realising it, is cruel. Because I will always want to be with you and I will always think I'm in love with you. And making me believe that you feel the same when you don't, it isn't fair.

Please, if you don't feel the same. Please let me forget. At this point I don't know how long my life will be, or how long I will fight for, but I need to start making it a happy one, and if you don't want to be part of it then that has to be it.

I wish you the happiest life possible."

Trying to breathe properly I re read the message over and over again and with shaking hands I pressed send.

I decided I deserved to be loved; I had never really believed that I did before. I had spent so long working so hard and abusing myself for other people's approval. It was time to turn that around. The next few days I felt like Bridget Jones when she quits her job and tells Daniel Cleaver that she'd "rather have a job wiping Saddam Hussein's arse" than be near him. R-E-S-P-E-C-T played in my head over and over; I had won. It was a little battle in the grand scheme of things but for the first time in years I felt free from Sam and my unrequited love. It felt fantastic.

Twenty Two

2012

Being in day treatment soon felt normal again for me. I got used to the hour drive to get there. I was comfortable with the people around me and I knew what each day brought. I soon found that the people I met there gave me more therapy than the programme most days; Millie was my DT angel who always knew when I was sad, when I needed to talk or when I just needed a cuddle. Heather was my surrogate big sister who was a constant source of kindness and a big softy with those she was close to but a Rottweiler if necessary to those who crossed her. Heather's bad language and sarcastic tone made me love her even more because she was so honest and would never pussy foot around a situation. If something was "fucking shit" she'd tell you about it. Out of the rest of the group of twelve I gelled with two others closely and they couldn't be two more different people; Isabelle was a South African beauty, tall, dark featured and indescribably beautiful. She started a few days after I did and I immediately warmed to her. Isabelle was well spoken, clever and exhibited a fierce confidence that seemed to assure herself and her place in the world. She had a beautiful family and the only faltering point she had that I could see was that she was stuck in this place with us. During the first few weeks she would not shy away from arguing back or standing up for herself. She was a little firecracker and completely changed the despondent dynamic of the group - a breath of fresh air. Marie was eight years older than me with a son and had had a completely different life to Isabelle. The age difference however seemed like nothing and her brilliant humour shined through and seemed to envelop me in a massive hug every time she laughed. She was beautiful in a non-conventional way but her eyes gave away the myriad of sadness that she felt. Both women had bulimia as well as anorexia; they were the first people I'd met in treatment that were like me so there was instantly a common bond. When Isabelle spoke of her eating disorder however, I felt a strength and an urge to fight against it, for her daughter, her husband, her marriage, her life; that I didn't detect in Marie. Marie seemed resigned to her life despite the sadness it brought her. There was a feeling that she wouldn't be able to change even if she wanted to. It was a rare occurrence that she was positive about her efforts but when she was I would try to cling on to the hope that she too could get better. I had the honour to know each of them; to see them in their good days and their bad days, support them and love them no matter what. I didn't see them as damaged, or mentally unstable. All I saw were four beautiful women, stunning in their own ways, all with hearts of gold, all plagued with an illness that was unbelievably hard to recover from. It wasn't fair.

I sat in the usual circle of blue cushioned chairs and surveyed the rest of the group. Some young, some old, some with children, some with jobs that were so high up they couldn't talk about them, some that were also recovering alcoholics as well as anorexics. Some had been ill for thirty years, some for only one; so many people from so many different backgrounds and walks of life. There's no truth in the phrase that 'eating disorders are only for middle class girls who have nothing better to do than concentrate on their looks'. That kind of bullshit is spouted out into society by someone that has no experience behind the dirty curtain of eating disorder treatment. They see statistics and assume without knowing the reality or bothering to find out.

A prime argument against this stereotype was a man in his forties who was part of our group. He scared me at first; ashamed as I was to admit it, purely because I had never met a man with an eating disorder. Matt was tall, bone thin with a weathered face and covered in tattoos. A recovering alcoholic with two children and a supportive wife, he had spent time in prison and circled with the wrong crowd for a lot of his life. My fear of him was soon extinguished when I realised how kind and genuine he was and he brought a new dynamic into the group which is so badly needed in treatment. Matt was funny and supportive. As with a lot of men he found sharing how he felt and how he was coping hard, and most of his struggles were documented instead on paper inside the daily 'food and mood' sheets we had to fill out. Matt wanted to get better, he had a reason to for his children, but as with most patients wanting to get better is one thing but actually recovering is another.

I found the food really hard to cope with, harder than I expected, despite my determination. The portion sizes were a lot bigger than in The Abbey and having to eat every last bite sent my reflux into overdrive. After each meal I would be battling to keep the food down and it got worse after every Fortisip and every snack. To try to relieve this horrible side effect of eating, I continued to skip everything that I was able to outside of treatment, which in reality was a very bad idea. The whole point of Day Treatment was to get back into a normal eating pattern so that you are less likely to binge and more likely to restore your beaten down metabolism. I knew I was kicking myself in the face by not adhering to the pattern but I just couldn't face having to swallow sick for an entire day. When I was at The Abbey and they saw how I struggled, the doctor told me that I may have damaged my body. There is a lower sphincter at the bottom of your oesophagus just above your stomach that lets food in and stops acid from coming back. They thought mine was either corroded away from the acid when I had been sick for so long or just weak and too used to letting food go both ways. Once in Day Treatment I started to pursue this; if I could have an operation that would physically stop me from being sick then I would have no choice to get better. Then the hardest part would be eating in the first place and that seemed a lot better than what I had to go through every time I ate something. I prayed that there was something wrong with me physically, something that could be fixed and wasn't just my screwed up brain ruining everything. I was booked in for a gastroscopy at the hospital; it was the first time I had been to a medical hospital since Turkey. As I walked through the doors of the ward I realised that I was unbelievably tensed up. I looked around - no blood on the floors, the beds looked pretty clean and I was almost certain that the toilets in Cheltenham wouldn't be holes in the ground. I breathed out, unclenching my hands and letting my shoulders relax. It would be okay here. The procedure was simple enough. They had to shove a tube down my throat to check the sphincter and my stomach for any damage. It wasn't a dangerous operation; I'd be given some anaesthetic so I wouldn't feel anything and I'd be allowed home that day. Easy. Most of my time at the hospital was a blur, I remember going into the operating room and being thankful that I wasn't being strapped down naked this time. Then there was the anaesthetic that wasn't supposed to put me to sleep but I must have, as the next thing I remember was waking up to my father and stepmother beside my bed. As I left the hospital and walked out into the December air I thought, "Another successful trip to hospital, maybe I'm getting the hang of this…" then realised what a stupid thing that was to think, chided myself, shook my head and made a promise to myself that I'd never be back.

Twenty Three

After a few days, I got my results.... there was
nothing wrong with me. Any normal person
might be overjoyed by this news; it meant their
body wasn't irreversibly damaged, that they could
just work harder to get better and no surgery was
needed, but for me I was devastated. My journey
to recovery was going to be even harder now. It
was all down to me and no medical operation
could make it better. I carried on with the
mundane routine of Day Treatment; most days
we were expected to have breakfast and our
morning snack at home before we came in, then
once we were in session we would either have
CBT groups, discussion groups, an open group if
anyone was struggling or if it was weigh day we
would have weight feedback, where we would be
expected to announce if our weight had gone up,
down or stayed the same and then explain how it
made us feel. These sessions would be broken up
by lunch, which consisted of a hot cooked meal
with a dessert; afternoon snack, which had the
choice of nuts, a chocolate bar, a cake or
something of that sort, followed with a piece of
fruit. Then finally it would be dinner time which

was either soup with bread or sandwiches and a piece or fruit. Each meal or snack meant that we all sat around tables at specific times of the day with a specific time to eat it by. Everyone had to finish and no behaviours were allowed.

Behaviours come in all shapes and forms. Some people would excessively tap their feet or shake their legs, others would eat one type of food at a time: for example vegetables first, then meat, then potatoes with no mixing of food at all. Some would cut their food into tiny mouse sized pieces; others would pour salt and pepper excessively so that the food wouldn't be enjoyable anymore. There are hundreds of ways that behaviours take form and the staff could identify all of them. I was a leg shaker. I would need to be constantly moving and I had never realised that I couldn't sit still until I started treatment. Maybe it was a way that made me feel safer-like all other behaviours? Maybe I was just a fidget? Who knows? All I knew was that it was incredibly hard to stop something that you didn't even know you did!

Our group was very mixed. Over the weeks we had a few people come for a day and either run away or break the stone solid rules of Browns. If anyone was sick between meals then it meant an immediate dismissal. One girl just couldn't handle the food in her stomach and slyly slipped away from group and threw up. She was made to sit in front of us and tell us what she had done; the fear in her eyes and the sadness on her face reminded me of being a child and being really told off by your parents. It felt wrong. A lot of treatment felt like that, it was like we had to be degraded from adults into children so we could learn how to have a healthy relationship with food again. Some days this digression back into feeling like a child angered me, others it was comforting, as though things could all be made better by a cuddle and kind words. Unfortunately, people don't recover from addictions and illnesses with a cuddle. If only.

However I got through each day. Some I would spend battling with my inner demons, others I would concentrate on getting my friends there to talk, and sometimes we'd even laugh. We'd paint cups, colour in drawings and have quizzes, fully immersing ourselves in the digression to being kids again. Millie and I would always have the funniest conversations and find a way to giggle through our pain; once when I was playing The Sims on my laptop to pass the time, Millie told me that when she used to play it she found a cheat so that her character never had to eat.

There was a pause as we looked at each other; "Millie…even your Sims were anorexic" and we started to laugh. We laughed and couldn't stop laughing until we cried.

There was a bump in the road where one of my old school friends joined the staffing team as a trainee mental health nurse. The humiliation I felt at the fact that she had continued on in her life to be a healthy, successful and happy individual that ended up caring for me was so embarrassing I could cry, but I soon discovered that school peers or not, she was amazing at her job and was a value to any clinic she worked in. After a few weeks I felt used to the environment. I had a group of people I would spend time with every day and we could always rely on each other when we were struggling.

On the outside things were good. Inside though I wasn't coping. The food I was being forced to eat was too much and every day when I left I would throw up in some part of the forest on my way home. I started to lie in my food diaries and pretended that I wasn't throwing up as much as I was. The staff believed I was getting better and talk soon turned to the inevitable; when I should be discharged.

Of course, I wasn't ready. I was far from it. The sheer panic I felt in leaving and having to get on with my life was too much for me. I did a great job of pretending that things were fine and that I was coping, but really I was like a swan; calm and collected on the surface but underneath the water my legs were going full throttle. I was frantically paddling, trying to stop myself from drowning in hate and illness, waiting for the day that my body would not fight for me to keep me alive any longer.

Twenty Four

During those months in day treatment my
relationship with Marc had started to take a
downwards turn. Despite my liberation from Sam
I still hadn't learnt to stand up for myself
romantically. I had visited him once after I was
released from the Abbey and it was almost
perfect; we sat, talked and laughed, we told each
other our struggles that were still ongoing. After
his first relapse when we were both inpatients, he
seemed to be doing a lot better, but it became
clear to me that his past relationships had really
damaged him and he no longer trusted women to
accept him for who he was. I had thought that I
was the exception to this rule. I felt like I knew
him and he knew me, I didn't care about any of
his insecurities because to me he was the boy who
accepted my faults and cared for me despite them.
Thats what love was, wasn't it? We went for a
walk over the hills near the Abbey and looked
over Bristol as the day turned to night and the
view became littered with stars and lights. We
kissed and it was no longer against the rules. We
were free to be with each other fully without any
guilt or consequences. I was free, I was risky and

unabandoned. I felt liberated.

That night we had dinner with one of the alcoholics, Richard, and his wife and if I hadn't had all the memories of being force fed in that place it would have almost been flawless. I left him that night feeling dizzy with all these emotions that I hadn't felt for so long and the excitement of the opportunity of feeling loved once again. He visited me in the forest and we chatted and laughed and I felt myself falling for this imperfect, messed up yet amazing person. We could be great together. We could be something spectacular and I could be better. Little did I know that would be one of the last times that I ever saw him.

When Christmas 2012 came and I started to struggle with the fears of the massive amounts of food and the pressure to be better for my family, I arranged to drive to Cardiff on Boxing Day to see him. Christmas was difficult. I wanted to show my family that I was happy and getting better so that they didn't need to worry about me anymore, I needed to hide the pain and torment inside as well as the disappointment within myself that I wasn't strong enough to recover. On Christmas Eve I cried myself to sleep; I wasn't worthy of the amazing family I had around me, how could I be when I was jealous of them and when all I wanted was for my eating disorder to kill me so I didn't have to fight anymore? Christmas Day was the same as usual. Mild arguments, too much food and me finding any opportunity to go and throw up in-between eating. I drank to try and dull the pain inside me, half hoping that I would get so drunk that I would confess that things weren't as great as they seemed. My control and guilt got the better of me, as always I stayed silent and instead woke up with a massive headache the next day.

With a huge hangover and even bigger butterflies, I started my journey to see Marc on the afternoon of Boxing Day. I had bought him a bag full of presents so that maybe he would realise how much I cared for him and drove to Cardiff, constantly questioning what I was playing at and what kind of lovesick girl I had become all the way there. I must have got through a pack of cigarettes on the way over just to try and calm my nerves.

I used to hate smoking. My family in general don't smoke and my sisters have always hated it. My brother Drew however smoked from a young age, much to my mother's disgust, and the smell of old smoke on clothes always used to remind me of him. It was comforting and always made me happier.

I didn't smoke my first cigarette until I was about fifteen; I had moved to Malvern and became friends with a group of people that were slightly rebellious in school. Most of them smoked but I could quite easily be around it without getting curious. It wasn't until that first night I got drunk off some terrible cider at my friend Beth's house that I had my first drag. Beth was a bit different from everyone else at school, she often had to take days off when she wasn't well but I was so drawn to her because she was artistic, fun, genuine, kind and had such a brilliant laugh that was infectious. My best friend Louise had introduced me to her group of friends and Beth was one of them. Our group was called the 'Randomers' by the more popular clan and although I came into school in year ten and was lucky enough to be friends with people from most cliques, they were the ones that made me feel most accepted as I was. The boys were kind, fun and a completely different species from the ones that had made my life hell in my previous school. The girls were funny, beautiful and had so much depth and intelligence in them they instantly became some of my closest friends.

It was crazy just how much my life had changed since I had left school; I hadn't seen my old friends in years and was now sitting in the car on my way to an ex-cocaine addicts house that I had only really spent time with in a mental hospital.

Another drag, calm down...

Beth's family had become my surrogate family in Malvern; my mum had to work long shifts and although our relationship had improved, we were no longer constantly arguing like we did when we first moved, I always wanted to be out with my friends. Beth's mum and dad fostered children so they were used to lots of people in their house and every single time I was there they would welcome me with open arms. Although I loved my father, Beth's became like a foster dad to me; I could laugh and mess around with him and I got away with murder. Beth's mum was loving, kind but also didn't take any crap from anyone, which I admired fully. They allowed us to drink if we wanted to, smoke with them whilst chatting and watching TV; it was a home away from home, and I loved it. It was at Beth's that I had my first drag of a cigarette. I hated it and I hated myself for doing something I had always told myself that I would never do. After that first drag however I had already lost my moral high ground - not to mention the £100 bet my brother would give me if I reached 21 without smoking - so I stopped caring and started smoking with my friends. Then I started to enjoy it, five years later and I was a full on smoker…whoops.

I arrived at Marc's Nans' house. My hands were sweaty and I had to check my face twice for any untoward snot or make up disasters. Once he opened the door all my fears and nerves disappeared. There was the boy that accepted me and understood me, with a smile on his face and his arms welcoming me into him. That night we lay together and talked about how we were both doing since leaving The Abbey. I fell asleep in his arms only to wake up in the morning questioning if we were really just friends or something more. When we were together I felt happy. We laughed and we talked openly and honestly, but there was something that seemed to stop him from kissing me one too many times or holding me for too long. I left Cardiff the next day after spending the morning with him, going over our few hours together and wondering if I was doing something wrong.

After that day I didn't see him again. He started lying to me about benign and insane things and then would go quiet. He'd tell me that he had no money to see me, that he was getting operations on his junk, that he slept with another man- the last absolutely flooring me. A few days later he would confess that he had been lying and we'd continue in the same vein as before until he would lie again.

My heart, which still felt broken after Sam, felt chipped at once again, how foolish I was for letting someone in. I was being emotionally bombarded with anger and disappointment and I started to look to myself as the reason why he was behaving the way he was. It was my fault - I was too damaged, I was too damaged to be with anyone, why would someone like him want to be with the ugly duckling. Fairy tales didn't exist and my happy ending certainly didn't. I was revolting. The eating disorder stepped back in well and truly at that point; I saw it as my saviour to take me away from the pain of once again not being good enough for someone. I was ill and I was good at it, no one else could touch me now.

A few weeks later, in 2013, I was discharged from day treatment. Although my mind was a lot worse than when I started again at Browns, my weight was restored and I was officially meant to go back into Cognitive Behavioural Therapy. I was broken once more. The few days that I had managed not to throw up in The Abbey were a thing of the past and I no longer knew how to deal with eating a meal and not throwing up. I hated everything about myself. I hated Marc for ignoring me. I hated food in general. I hated my family for loving me and caring about me because all I wanted to do was be invisible, be dead, and not be able to feel anything. I stopped trying and within a few weeks I had lost over a stone and was at risk of being sent to hospital once more.

Twenty Five

2013

The sky started to become my great healing point.
It's funny, I didn't believe in God or any higher
power growing up and my thoughts on the
afterlife were often confused. I don't believe in
heaven or hell and yet whenever I look up at the
night sky, I pick a star and see my Nanny. I talk to
her, ask for advice or just tell her my fears, hopes
and dreams, wishing she was here again. I often
stand outside and just look up, getting lost in the
infinite magnitude of the universe that we live in.
The moon fascinates me, the faces and pictures
that you can decipher inside it, the way that it
paints rainbows on any clouds passing beneath it
and the fact that it can be obscured by a dark
cloud purely made up of water vapour. It's
beautiful and illogical and incandescent all at the
same time. When I looked up at the sky it calmed
and soothed me. On the nights where I no longer
wanted to be part of the earth or part of life itself
it showed me that the world is a beautiful place
and all I need to do is participate within it to
emanate that beauty within myself. I could be

beautiful in a way that I had never known, I was allowed to be strong and pure, to find my own light and bathe in it.

On the nights where the clouds covered every part of the sky, when I wasn't talking to my nanny in the stars, I was writing letters to her;

"Dear Nanny,

Just writing those words makes me miss you even more. Knowing that you'll never read this or be able to respond to me again still hurts so much even though it's been over a year...

I wish every day that you could write one more letter or send me one more sign. I saw you in the robins, in the feathers, in the Emperor butterflies that were all over the church on the way of your memorial service, that still appear in unexpected places - but the feathers have stopped since I've had my tattoo and now the closest I get are dead birds!

If you could see me now I really wonder what you'd think — I imagine you being so disappointed with how I seem to attempt to ruin my life at every hurdle and how weak I am to seem unable to get over this horrible illness. This horrible eating disorder. Ella says that you'd be sad — like everyone else is, sad that you can't help and that I'm struggling. That makes it worse though. The thought of you sad is heart-breaking. When I think of you, sad and scared and so removed from the person you once were, it feels like there's a gaping black hole inside me. I'll never forget your screams when you fell down the stairs, the fear of breaking your leg again or the way that you and Grampy, for what seemed like the first time, couldn't comfort each other or make everything better. I hate the thought of you feeling so detached and so alone and I wish most of all I knew what you were thinking…I could have asked, just like I could have just walked through a door and seen you alive that one last time on the day you died, but I couldn't because I was too scared. I am so sorry. I'd do anything to change things but I know that I can't and I'll live with that decision for the rest of my life…

Seeing you in the hall afterwards, you just looked asleep. Even though you had become so unbelievably thin and your hair wasn't the long beautiful hair that I had grown up knowing, you were still my nanny. I could have laid there with you for hours just stroking your hair. Your warmth had all gone and you changed colour right in front of my eyes, but I was never scared then which is so odd because you dying was the scariest thing that had ever happened. But you were still my Nanny. You still are.

That day was one of the last days we were one big family, it's scary how quickly we broke apart without you. I've tried hard to keep us together and sort it out but I don't think I can do it anymore. It's still hard to believe that Grampy got married to someone else 8 months after you died. I don't think some people can forgive him for moving on so quickly. Would you? I hope so….I think so…but I don't know. Am I doing the right thing by trying to accept it or am I doing wrong by you?

You said in your letter to me when I went to Australia "you are only young once" and I keep trying to remind myself of that every day. Every day I carry on with this eating disorder is another day wasted. But I don't feel young anymore. I feel old. You dreamt about going me going to Drama School when I did. You believed in me so much and always said you could see me playing Eponine in Les Mis. I wish you could. I wish that I still could. I wish that I could make you proud of me again because right now you couldn't be. Not like this.

I want one last conversation with you, so you can snap me out of it. I feel as though nothing can. Even when they told me I'd most probably die before long if I didn't sort it…part of me didn't care. Is that selfish? I wanted that. It was easier to. It would mean the ultimate escape.

I feel like I'm climbing up a large grassy hill when it's raining and although I want to get to the top, I've slipped so many times. What if I'm not strong enough?

I wish you were here for a cuddle or a bad joke or to laugh. Your laugh was fantastic. Your smile just lit everything up. People exaggerate how amazing a person is once they're dead but with you I never will. You couldn't be exaggerated if I tried. You were my rock- someone with so much love and generosity in her heart. That's the person I strive to be like.

I love you so much….I wish you could tell me it back.

I miss you. x"

Writing was the only way I could say how I felt. I didn't want to tell my family and drag them down with me when they thought I was getting better. I was in so much pain physically, emotionally and mentally. I wanted to die but I wanted to live. I wished to be someone else but I was scared to leave the familiarity of the eating disorder. Depression was pulling me under and I wasn't sure if I wanted to sink into the darkness or fight against it. I was so confused. In the worst moments I started to forget what I loved about the world and the only time I managed to remember was when I saw a member of my family laugh or when the sunset was so unbelievably beautiful or the stars littered the sky with light. Those were the times that confused me most though; I didn't understand why I was pushing away a life that had the potential to be so beautiful. Although I was a grain of sand in a vast ocean of life I was important, I had to be. The stars made me feel inadequate and infinitesimal but because of them my existence was made up of stardust, of beauty. The only problem was that I had let self-hate, anger, pain and darkness in and because I didn't have the energy to fight it off, I was slowly becoming nothing but blackness and sadness.

How did I come back from it? How would more treatment help? How could I ever change the sadness in my heart?

My only constant was the sky and my hope.

The hope that one day I could truly laugh at the world and feel part of it.

NEVER MY AIM.

If death can end a love that once was true

and any trace of love be quickly shed,

then cast my faith from ever loving you,

ban thoughts of trust from trespassing my head.

For lust can blur the fondest lovers' eyes,

loneliness will canker all true reason,

no time is spent as patience would deny

any thought to recognise hearts treason.

So fondest thoughts are all too soon erased,

and first love questioned behind lovers back,

while they do sink to new arms of embrace

forgetting she that caused his heart to crack.

Forever now I'll lock my heart away, forever denying
false loves decay.

Written in 2012.

Twenty Six

2013

I found myself in darkness again. My world was black with hate and pain and although I could see glimpses of what life was like on the outside of the bubble I was encased in, I was never able to experience it fully. Part of me wanted to go back to hospital because I knew that I was safe there and there was no choice but to get better, but the other part wanted to hold on to my eating disorder. It wasn't until I started my sessions with Jodie, my Cognitive Behavioural Therapy councillor, that I found the true reasons.

CBT was something I didn't want to return to as I had felt that I had failed the process of recovery so badly and it was only going to go wrong. For the first few weeks I was grumpy and unwilling to speak. I let my thoughts and hatred of myself and my body cloud anything that was said to me and all I would let myself pay attention to was the falling number on the scale. I had so much shooting around in my head; confused feelings of wanting to fight and wanting to lay down and succumb to illness, wanting to say everything I was feeling and yet being able to say nothing. Most of the time wanting to be anorexic instead of bulimic, so that I could at least be thin and miserable. Yet I had glimpses of hope that I could be happy again if I just got my act together. But how? None of it made sense. Jodie wouldn't understand me anyway, how could she when I barely did?

I had arrived at one of my appointments one day just as my old day treatment crew came back in from lunch out. Lunch and snack out was a weekly dread for us, it would alternate weekly whether we had lunch or snack. I used to think that lunch out was the worse of the two as we weren't allowed safe foods like salad or low calorie options but after an experience in a local gardening shop cafe with our group, the youngest people in there surrounded by over 60's, an hour of anxiety, high tensions, tears and a panic attack, I decided that snack out was definitely worse. I always felt so vulnerable when I went out with day treatment on these occasions. It wasn't shame of being seen in public with the group of people I went with, in fact some of the girls and I were unbelievably close, it was the stares we seemed to attract and it made me feel more self-conscious about eating in public. The whole point of us going was to banish our fears of eating in restaurants and cafes and get over not knowing what was in our food or being in control of how it was made. To an extent regular challenges did help, but the problem I felt, was other people and the pressure not to have a meltdown when a massive plate of food was put in front of you.

When you are out with a noticeably ill group of people, others think that it is okay to stare at them and what they are eating with a complete disregard to how they are making anyone feel. Maybe it is the shock and realisation that thin people eat? Or just the fact that a tiny girl in front of them is eating and finishing a portion that they may not. Or maybe it's pure curiosity and I was paranoid. Be that as it may, every now and then when I was struggling with eating something I never normally would and could feel eyes directed towards our table, I felt the urge to stand up and just shout, "do you want to take a picture? It lasts longer". That or just act like a crazy person, throw my plate at them which would eliminate them staring at me as well as the food I had to eat. Two birds with one stone and all that.

There's a scene in 'Girl Interrupted' when

the group go out to an ice cream parlour and there's an altercation with the character Winona Ryder plays and a woman. When threatened, the whole group rally around Winona and act properly crazy; barking like dogs, singing, acting up to their 'mentally unstable' stereotype. It's hilarious. Sometimes that is all I wanted to do whenever someone stared at us or made some comment, just for the laughs..." think I'm crazy? You have no idea, let me show you just how mental I can be". My self-consciousness and logical brain however always held me back from these urges. Pity.

My days of lunch and snack out were behind me now though, I no longer had to conform to any rules or be forced to put anything into my mouth and I certainly hadn't- that was probably the cause of all the concerned faces I saw as my friends walked through the door of day treatment.

I didn't understand the looks that I got from them until years later when Millie and I sat down for coffee and she explained, "I was scared, you had got so tiny and you'd only been gone from day treatment a few weeks. I thought you were going to die..."

Back then I was oblivious to it. I didn't see a thin girl, I saw a greedy repulsive one that was just worthless in every way. After a brief chat, Jodie came out of her office to call me in for my appointment and begrudgingly I left the girls and went into yet another pointless CBT session.

I walked into the plain, cold room which they had attempted to improve with blue chairs and a potted plant that was actually wilting in the corner – ironic. It was that time again to be weighed and once again the needle dropped and I felt slightly elated. Jodie sat down and waited for me to put my layers back on (I needed them for comfort as well as warmth- I was constantly freezing) and sit in the square chair opposite. I always sat in the same position, legs up and knees into my body with my arms wrapped around them. It was my protected stance; no one could look at me properly.

Her eyes searched mine and she asked how I felt about my weight. I shrugged and said I didn't know really, I guess I was pleased.

She asked if I felt like I could help myself to

get better and when I replied I wasn't sure, that was when the threat of The Abbey was reintroduced.

I knew that Jodie was only trying to help and part of me wanted to go back but somewhere in me the penny dropped and I realised what my life was becoming.

Incessant sadness fell over me daily. I could never look in the mirror and feel content. I would let people walk over me and the only relief I would have would be visits to hospital - which could become a frequent occurrence if nothing changed. That or I would die. It was still a real possibility: My cramping hands and feet kept getting worse because of my dropping potassium levels and my heart felt fast but weak inside my chest.

What was the use of it all? Why was I letting myself go through the motions and pretending to get better instead of actively pursuing a new life?

I looked back at the years and saw a life

overridden by illness; solitude, failed relationship after failed relationship, relying too heavily on what others thought and said about me, being sick on my birthdays, unable to keep down the cake or the celebration meal. Being sick at my sister's wedding, my Nans funeral, my Nans memorial - every big moment of my life since my eating disorder started up till then was tarnished and it was all because of me. I thought of what I had done to my family and how I had scared everyone into treating me differently and how I had cut them out to try and lessen the pain of leaving them, and for the first time in a long time, I cried. I let the tears fall from my face and got every complicated, stupid thought out of my head and into the silent room for Jodie to hear.

After I had no more tears to cry and I had managed to control my breathing, I looked up and saw Jodie looking at me. She looked pained slightly by what I had just said but there was also a light in her eyes that made me feel there was some kind of hope.

"This sounds like it all started a long time ago" she said. "Do you know when? Do you know how?"

I looked at the floor and shook my head like a school girl ashamed at her lack of knowledge in a lesson.

"Well then this is what we need to work on. Normally we don't look back as it can be detrimental and we want you to move forward and past this illness, but I think if we can work out where it all started then maybe we can understand a bit more. We can then work to letting go of those thoughts and feelings that you have grown up with."

We sat for the rest of the hour compiling a list of things that happened over the course of my childhood that affected who I was now. There were points where I found continuing hard; remembering my time with Sam, re-living the death of my Nan, losing my dream of being an actress, my purpose. But with Jodie's' support, by the end of the session we had completed it and there was finally logic to this completely illogical person that I had become and it was all written down on paper.

"Events and Circumstances (that might

have sensitised me to my shape, weight and eating)

AGE 10 – 13 (up to a year before the onset of problem):

Found parents' divorce hard and often blamed myself

Used to call my math teacher my 'school daddy' – felt like I was replaced by my stepmother and my dad didn't need me anymore

Didn't get into the school my sisters did and didn't feel good enough or clever enough

Was called "turkey neck" by my sisters and became very self-conscious of it, felt left out

Bullied in secondary school – became more aware of what I looked like

Wanted to run away and wrote in my diary "wish I was dead" most days

Thought if I was "gorgeous" I'd be able to get a boyfriend – thought I needed one for male approval

Talked down to myself constantly out loud and in my diaries "I am so much uglier than any of my friends"

Cutting myself with scissors and knives

AGE 14- 15 (twelve months before onset):

Started to write down what I ate — kept vowing to eat just fruit and skipping breakfast and lunch

Hated myself — talked myself down when I ate too much, told myself I was fat and ugly

Started looking into exercise as a way to change how I looked

Had a certain view to what "fit" looked like — saved photos from magazines and off the internet to keep me inspired

Thought I couldn't be happy unless I was thin

Being at a new school with a new start gave me the motivation to try to be accepted and liked

Lots of arguments with my mum — felt angry a lot of the time

Uncomfortable with relationships — was taught that sex was wrong and bad and something to be afraid of

Still ate what I classed as "bad food" and then beat myself up for it

Felt like a spare part — not beautiful

Started to restrict and trying to starve myself

14th August 2006 — first made myself sick.

Self-criticised constantly — all or nothing thinking

Felt confused as I was happy with my friends and my life apart from my relationship with my parents.

AGE 16-17 (the twelve months after the onset):

Met Sam - I thought I was in love.

Felt unwanted by parents

Tired all the time, slept a lot

Smoked more, skipped school, started drinking and smoking weed with my friends – wanted to escape and live dangerously to forget about how I felt

Other people's actions influenced how I treated myself

Negative mind-set

Still ate takeaways every now and then but felt "huge" afterwards

Hardly ate if I could get away with it, kept trying to starve

If I ate more I'd be sick which started becoming more and more regular.

Felt inexperienced sexually because I was scared – worried that I was the reason I was alone

Felt average, ordinary, plain, boring, nothing special

Appendicitis: ruined my incessant sit ups, ugly scar, unable to move much

Still happy with my friends despite it

AGE 18-21 (since then):

Unstable relationship with Sam — caused me to doubt myself more and more, persuaded myself it was how I looked

Felt ill a lot of the time

Arguments with mum made me feel bad

Dieted, avoided eating anything, thought I ate too much and hated myself for being weak, wrote down everything I ate and being sick made me feel a lot better

Felt alone a lot of the time

Used to hit myself, kept a lot of secrets and blamed myself for everything

One of my best friends descended into anorexia — felt a mixture of jealousy and fear for her, wanted her to be happy again

Walked out of lessons, rushed in and out of relationships — never let anyone get close to me

Threw up after nearly all meals, hated being hungry but didn't want to eat and would only have brief periods of eating normally when I was happy

Used to walk for miles, went to the gym every day for 2 hours at least, measured my body and obsessed about weight, counted calories

Became unbelievably organised and a neat freak which changed my personality completely

Spent a lot of time alone, binging increased

Found out my Nan was ill which made me realise what I was doing and want to get better for the first time

Didn't sleep well, felt faint a lot, exhausted and weak but pushed myself harder in the gym

Went to Australia and was happy - I fitted into a size zero, so busy that food became less important for me although I missed going to the gym

Started rearranging food (mine and other peoples) and needed it to be in order

Started uni – enjoyed being the fittest and felt competitive, exercise became secretive, 4am runs

Moved in with nan and lived with my sister, lots of arguments and tension, avoided eating with others

Binging increased, self-hate got worse

Saw nanny stop eating and joined her, wanted to take the pain away, wanted to make her better

Nanny died, nothing else mattered, wanted to die too."

And there it was, right in front of me.

Nearly my entire life set out in bullet points. A map of my journey and the reasons for the person that was sat in a square blue chair in a cold room, being treated for an eating disorder. Being treated but not actively taking part in trying to get better and for the first time I knew why. I knew the answer, the cause and the remedy. I understood.

Seeing each step of my life mapped out before me there was an overwhelming voice screaming out of it. It was the voice of my ten-year-old self reciting something into a pillow that I had long since forgotten and yet had entwined into every sense of my being. The words that I had believed and told myself every day for over ten years.

The words; "**I'm not good enough**".

We often carry with us emotional baggage and beliefs which weigh us down and cause physical and emotional turmoil. My central belief of "I'm not good enough" had caused me to seek fulfilment and satisfaction externally. This led me to pursuing acting, where I could get the immediate gratification of performing well and getting applause once I'd finished- making me feel important and feeding my ego. It also led me to trying to fill myself up from the outside in though; food, boys, clothes sizes, calories, numbers - anything that could be physically there and that I could see a kind of progress in a sense was being used to try to make me feel fulfilled.

Twenty Seven

Love is a funny thing. It is so diverse and ever changing; it can make you giddy, happy, blind, sad, jealous, angry. It can make the sun seem that little bit brighter or break your soul piece by piece. When I was 16 I thought I had found the meaning of it; I had watched the films, I had read the books, I had performed the play. Being with Sam made me feel like my life was perfect but when I was without him and it was over I experienced just how   devastating it can feel. He had the ability to make me feel like the most beautiful person in the world as well as the ugliest. And I let him. I had already grown up aware of relationships and how horrible they are when they end. My parents divorced when I was 7. It broke me and I had to watch them arguing over money, me and my sisters, how to parent; but no matter how hard I tried I couldn't make it better. As the youngest I was the last one left that house hopped between my Dad and his new wife and my mother. I was the one that was the reason for the arguments I saw. Things stuck in my head over the years; my mother crying, my stepmother ringing the police because my mum wanted to stay to talk to my dad who was shoving a door in her face, trying to make her leave. Hearing things that a young girl shouldn't, crying myself to sleep and being in the middle, feeling alone. After a while when I'd started secondary school, I couldn't handle living with my dad anymore and telling him so was horrendous. Even though I knew that he was sad I still questioned if he really loved me because I never felt like he fought for me.

My family life by my twenties was ten times better but I still had grown up hating marriage and being cautious about relationships. I never really had a proper boyfriend until I was in my late teens but by then my view of myself often ruined most relationships as I'd convince myself that they'd soon find someone better and leave. So I would be the one to end it before I could be the one to be hurt. As my mother had my older brother young, I had made a vow to myself never to lose my virginity until I was sixteen. In truth it wasn't that hard as I was petrified of sleeping with anyone. Through conversations with her in my teens, I believed that sex was a massive deal, it wasn't very nice and it was almost wrong. I never wanted anyone to touch me in case they wanted to sleep with me, so any boyfriend that I had was quickly dumped if I thought that the relationship was heading that way. I was scared and I was confused. I worried so much so that in the end my first time was with was my best friend at a party when I was so drunk I barely remember it. It ruined our friendship and took away one of the closest people I had, thus enforcing that sleeping with someone only leads to bad things. This fed my eating disorder as I believed that the way I was needed to change, but at that time I didn't have the tools to do it. I told myself that being thin would mean I would be more confident. I had no clue how wrong that statement was.

The first boy I thought I loved was Sam. It was amazing, exciting, bitter-sweet and devastating all at the same time. Seeing his smile, his lips playing with my name and his eyes looking into mine took me into a different world that I never wanted to leave. It was a love that I never got over. I had a few quick relationships after that; the complicated stoner who wrote me love songs but was useless at actually being there for me; the boy from France that was my best friend but who I felt was far too attractive to be seen with someone like me. The boy who was too old for me and the first one who dumped me first, leaving me crying in a graveyard until my best friends came and pacified me with alcohol and cigarettes; the boy who made Australia safe and familiar and taught me to say yes to life; the boy who my sisters nicknamed Mr Tumnus who was so kind, loving and took me for adventures but who I couldn't love back because of my cloud of depression. There were also boys like Ben who I could never work out; we met at my sister Ella's wedding and I spent well over a year craving to be with him and wanting him to want me too. But aside from a brief chance of hope, and a brilliant, yet slightly hung-over kiss the day after my twenty-first birthday, I had to accept that he just wasn't that into me and we became great friends instead. Each one taught me something about myself and acted as a learning curve, the only problem was whenever Sam came back; the boy who span me around to make me dizzy with laughter, who kissed me in the rain and promised to marry me one day, every feeling I had ever felt seemed a touch on the surface to my feelings for him. This was something that kept me ill, I still needed to be good enough for him to finally say yes and be with me, I needed him to love me back and so the eating disorder carried on entwining itself into my being and destroying any certainty I had as to who I was.

By the time I had come to my revelation in treatment, my relationship with Marc had come to a bitter end. His lies and the way he made me so uncertain had taken its toll on me and I realised that being with him would never make me better. He was keeping me ill. I started to concentrate on myself and the only boy that I completely trusted to share everything with was one of my sister Leila's friends. I had grown up knowing him but it was only in my late teens that we started to become friends. He and my sister were best friends and by my twenties knew me inside out and we used to spend a lot of time together. However, I was Midget Jones (a nickname coined in sixth form by my friends and a homage to Bridget because I was small and rubbish with men) and of course things got complicated.

We spoke more and more and both he and I started developing feelings for each other. It was confusing to know if it was just an unbelievably close friendship or the possibility of something fantastic, but at first I was just grateful that he was in my life and he accepted me for who I was. He text me every day I was in hospital, knew every single one of my doctors' appointments and always asked me how I was. As well as being supportive, he also knew when to take the piss out of me and make me laugh and our conversations mostly consisted of us poking fun at one another just because we could get away with it. After a while I started thinking that maybe this was what a relationship needed to work and we started talking about being together. I couldn't go behind my sisters back and so we asked her permission. It didn't go well. How he and I felt for each other managed to ruin everything, their over ten-year long friendship ended and for a time my sister refused to speak to me. We never tried to be together again and instead tried to get back to the friendship we had, but things were never the same and it got harder and harder to stay in touch so eventually another string in my support network was broken. I missed having one person that I knew accepted me. Relationships ruined everything.

I decided to focus on myself. I hated it. I was used to ignoring my feelings, ignoring my face in the mirror, pretending everything was ok, pretending I didn't care or just beating myself up, but with the help of regular sessions at the clinic and a lot of hard work, I started to really fight my eating disorder, and what's more I wanted to. Some days I would start to destroy all the work I put in by drinking multiple bottles of wine and staying away from everyone, eating everything I could see and purging until I saw blood. Other days I could take a grip on my recovery and start to work harder. There is no perfect recovery.

There is no way to do it right. There is only hard work and acceptance that at times you may have to take a step back before you can go forwards again. It's not easy and it never will be.

The main battle I had to fight was to overpower my belief that 'I wasn't good enough' and the only way that was possible was to start being kinder to myself. Every morning I would wake up and look at myself in the mirror and find 3 good things that I liked about myself. At first it felt ridiculous, juvenile even, and I couldn't find anything so I settled on things like 'I like my wrists' or 'I like my tattoo', but with time and repetition I started to really appreciate my body and what it had gone through and the fact that it hadn't given up on me when I had begged it to. I wasn't in love with it but neither was I constantly wishing it would look different. Acceptance is such a massive step and I was starting to take it. I could walk out the door and believe those three little things each day and, with time, my confidence started to grow. Instead of telling myself negative statements multiple times a day, I would recite affirmations in my head 'I deserve happiness', 'I can do whatever I put my mind to', 'I am good enough'. No matter how much I didn't believe them, I started to try to counteract every single negative that crept in with a positive.

As a society we don't ever concentrate on ourselves in a positive way. There are so many ifs and buts and when someone is proud of who they are and their achievements they are called self-satisfied or self-indulgent. We trained our way out of self-love and instead choose to berate ourselves.

When was the last time you appreciated yourself for you?

You as you are now?

There's always an; 'I'll be happy when this happens or that happens' and we never just accept ourselves or our situations and appreciate them. We can trust and we can love the skin we are in - it just takes time.

I started to understand it. My recovery was never perfect. I had grown up believing that I was good for nothing. I was cold. I was unloving. I was pointless. But every time I looked at the stars I saw my nanny. I saw my belief. I was made of the stardust and the stars enabled me to become whatever I needed to be. All I needed to be was strong enough to fight, and for the first time in so many years I saw the reason why I had to. It wasn't for anyone else. It was for me.

It isn't as easy as changing the mind-set that you are in however. I felt alone. I felt helpless. My friends were far away, distant, uncaring at times, and those closest to me didn't seem to understand. I wanted to get better but every step I took meant I was pushed back. Both mentally or physically. I started to wonder if I even wanted to survive the night or whether it was my time to leave the world now that I had chosen to fight against this illness, I sometimes didn't know if I even cared.   I carried on with my happy face though, my tears were for me only and no one could know the dilemma that I faced. Am I ready to die? Am I ready to get better? Confusion could rock around in my head for hours and I would lie in bed feeling my heart beating weakly, scared that it would give out at any second. Scared that it would carry on beating and I would have to face another day of struggle. And yet being able to touch every bone in my ribs made me feel proud? I was so messed up. I knew that this was the time though. This was my time to get better…

It was my time to raise two fingers in the air, smile and scream "This is me! And I'm going to love it!" no matter how hard it was going to be.

Twenty Eight

2013

The end of April announced the arrival of my 22nd birthday. CBT was emotionally exhausting but had helped me to keep my head above water. So much had changed in one year. Looking back at the nightmare of a 21st birthday and the year that followed on after, I was very glad that my 21st year on this earth was ending and the 22nd year was beginning

. My 21st started off well enough, I woke up with my best friend and we spent most of the day just chilling out together. I had organized a big party involving friends old and new and had spent hours preparing, I had a beautiful sparkly gold dress, a tan, fake eyelashes and had tried to get as skinny as possible by skipping as many meals as I could and throwing up whatever I ate. I think we started drinking not long after lunchtime. I was so excited getting ready and it was such a beautiful day, I remember feeling happy…which was quite rare at this point as it wasn't long after I had

collapsed at uni and had to leave. By this point
my Grampy had moved on and he now lived with
his new wife but I had my best friend Michelle
living with me so that's all that mattered as I
wasn't so alone. It wasn't until we left to go to the
party that things took an extreme turn for the
worse. My memory is pretty much blank as I
think the alcohol hit me on the way there, causing
me to arrive before everyone else, then think that
no one was coming because I had no friends. I
was plastered. I was plastered and all my family
that were there knew. Luckily none of my friends
had arrived before me so they didn't have to stand
there awkwardly as the birthday girl stumbled
around, pissed as a fart and sticking out like a sore
thumb. I was loud and slurring and constantly
trying to pull my dress up which was falling off
me, causing me to look extremely unladylike and
in short, a mess.

Things then went from bad to worse; I ended
up in the toilet crying with my oldest sister Ella.
She took me outside to sober up in the fresh air
but I didn't want to go back inside. I spouted a
load of rubbish out of my mouth, none of which
made sense, and I carried on being irrational and
refusing to go back inside to my party. My
Mother had come to try and reason with me as
well but nothing worked. I was adamant that I

didn't want to go back in because everyone at the party hated me and the swearing began. Usually I would never swear at my mother, not unless I wanted to risk my life, it was a very embarrassing moment that I will never repeat and one of my least proud moments…Even worse than farting really loudly in assembly when I was in year 4, then trying to blame it on the girl next to me. No one was convinced and for a while I was teased for being 'the girl that laughed so much she farted'.

My Mum and Ella realised that I hadn't eaten anything that day so tried to take me to a nearby fish and chip shop before my guests arrived and saw the extreme drunken mess that was the birthday girl…I however seemed to turn into someone else, someone I have rarely seen, thank god. I wanted to run away, yep that's right…I wanted to run away from chips…At this point I'm pretty sure I started telling everyone to "fuck off". I cried to both of them saying every evil, vile, depressed thoughts that were in my head. I was a mess. The alcohol had unlocked the beast in me and I have no recollection of what I said to them but the things I have been told disappoint, embarrass and sadden me. I think I was so lost in depression and my ED that once my senses had been blurred with alcohol, the barriers were thrown to the ground and everything came out at once. It was awful.

We sat in the car eating chips while Mum and Ella tried to make light of my drunkenness despite the depressive slurring coming from my mouth. They tried to persuade me normally, getting me to make sense about why I didn't want to attend my own 21st birthday party. Ella later told me she ended up getting so cross with me she shouted at me, she couldn't understand why I felt so rubbish and was frustrated that I wasn't having a wonderful time at my own birthday party. I was supposed to be happy but instead I had spent an hour crying. Ella was helpless and felt as though she had failed me as a sister. Knowing that I made her feel like that was awful, the effect that my eating disorder and my depression had on my family was devastating. A mental illness never just affects the sufferer, it affects the whole family and it can rip you all in two. I was never really aware what I was doing to my parents, my sisters, my brother, my cousins, my grandparents. I never really thought they had a clue, neither could I understand why they cared. Really though, all they could see was someone they loved slowly destroying themselves and they were unable to do anything but to watch, as I had become unrecognisable through sadness and pain.

After Ella shouted at me, I started to pull myself together. Somehow, I was calmed down and nearly ready to return to my own birthday party. By this point most of my guests had arrived... I did have friends after all! But my makeup had been ruined; my eyelashes had fallen off through tears, there were white patches around my eyes where my tan had rubbed off, my eyes were puffy and terrible. Not a good look.

As we went to walk in, Michelle who was equally drunk, came to my aid and as my mum tried to explain that she needed to get me in and sort my face out, Michelle spouted out 'fuck off, I'm a makeup artist!'. I have no recollection of this so it's only what I have been told, but I think my mother realised just how drunk we both were at the time and let it slide, but Michelle, like me will always be horrified that those words ever came out of her mouth...especially to my mum. With time though the story became funnier and funnier and years later Michelle and I laugh about it. This definitely was a disaster birthday.

The rest of the night got better. I mellowed out and started to enjoy myself. I still remember nothing even years later, but the photos say it all; there was no one there with dark skin so my eyes were covered up with a pale concealer which gave me a reverse panda effect to my face. In every shot my eyes are glazed and I have a ridiculous smile on my face which I can't look back on and feel ashamed. I was ill. I was a very ill girl who didn't know what to do with herself so just got absolutely wasted to rid herself of the pain and the worry about her birthday. It was sad but the ridiculousness of it all is almost funny.

Needless to say waking up on my 22nd felt so much better. This was the time for me to enjoy being alive and although things were a little difficult, there were so many things to be happy about, not only because I was waking up again with Michelle, but because my life had started to take a positive turn after I had adopted a positive attitude. I was taking part in life. I was taking chances and opportunities; I was doing things that scared me. I was diving fully into CBT and recovery and never let the setbacks push me to the ground for too long. I was starting to live. I was starting to get better.

Twenty Nine

2014

Learning to get better also meant that I had to learn to get to know me. I had spent so many years not really getting to know the person I was and instead I just ignored myself and concentrated on my eating disorder and making sure those around me were happy. Happy and oblivious.

Living back in Cheltenham in the other, unused side of the house that my Nanny and Grampy lived in without Nanny being there anymore was strange, but living with my best friend Michelle meant that I could experience living independently without the money issues. Everything was up to me, what I ate, what I did and although I'd already had that lifestyle from the age of eighteen I finally felt ready to take it. I didn't know who I was or what I liked. When I was ill I used to run miles and miles telling myself that I liked running...when I was getting better I realised I hated running, I used to go out clubbing and drink myself stupid no matter how awful I would feel about myself the day after telling myself that it was fun...when I was getting better I realised that I can have a good night without being drunk and that I'm literally the worst on a hangover.

Spending time using my own intuition and with the support of someone that loved and cared about me right in the place I was living, meant that I felt safe making mistakes and learning who I was. I still had major slip ups and problems with my recovery, but the main thing to concentrate on was finding out who I was, what I liked and never to give up. That was the new adventure.

Nights on my own either went really well or really badly. Sometimes I would drink myself to a stupor and pass out, others I would concentrate on what I enjoyed and distract myself from any negative thoughts or feelings through positive actions and tasks: I would sing for hours, dance like no one was watching, laugh at my own ridiculous jokes. I learnt to be me and I learnt to accept me. At times I could get frustrated with myself. One night I went out to a club and nearly had a panic attack because of the amount of people that surrounded me. Other times I couldn't handle it when people complimented me and would either disregard it or shoot their opinion down. It was only when I took a step back that I realised that by laughing in someone's face when they tell you that you look pretty is just downright rude, you are disregarding their feelings towards you which will in turn make them feel a bit rubbish and invalidated. It was one of the hardest things to do but I trained myself to smile, say thank you and try taking their opinion on board. I tried to live on instinct, I let myself respond naturally without over thinking things; sometimes it went well and others it didn't, but with each mistake I made I never beat myself up about it or berated myself for getting things wrong. I had spent too long doing that. Instead I would accept, learn and move on.

Understanding who I was, what I wanted and what I believed in was a massive part of the change in my life. I believed in beauty. I believed in life, love, honesty and acceptance. I hated people that belittled others; put themselves above the rest, who made people feel small, useless, inadequate or stupid. I had surrounded myself with negativity and as I started to become aware of my own I also became aware of other peoples. As a society we are so judgmental and hard on ourselves. We are never happy. There's always an

'I'll be happy when' and the line that we draw always seems to get further and further away. I looked at everything that surrounded me and all there seems to be is pressure surrounding us; pressure to do well in school, your learning, your job, and your relationships. Pressure to conform to having that perfect body, pressure to live an 'interesting' life, pressure to live the 'best life', pressure to look a certain way (despite the fact that this 'perfect look' changes every week). We are constantly fighting against something; whether it is banishing 'the last few pounds', working hard enough to get that promotion and unfortunately more and more we are starting to fight ourselves.

And for the first time in my life I asked myself "why?"

Why was it that I felt the need to conform to the rest of the world? To make myself miserable in order to fit into a box that I would never naturally fit into.

Growing up, the pressure I was under was massive and I personally believe that children and teenagers today have to cope with even more. As a society we judge each other on how we look before anything else. We unknowingly say critical comments about other people on TV or in magazines, we scrutinize ourselves and our bodies incessantly and who hears all this? Not just our subconscious mind but everyone around us; our friends, our family, our children. We feed negativity into each other. A lot of people say that media is to blame for the constant increase of eating disorders and mental illness in our society, but I truly think that we are partly to blame too because of the way in which we are conditioned. How do we expect to grow happy and healthy if all we are surrounded by is negativity?

This was when my 3 good things really helped me, as instead of being horrible and pessimistic all the time to myself and others, I had to try to focus on the good; even if some days it was difficult.

I use this technique now with the people that I coach. No matter how terrible the day has been or how rubbish you feel, having to find 3 good things to think about and write down makes so much of a difference. It's so hard to do for the first few days but creating this habit day by day, week by week, can totally transform your mindset into one that is positive and motivating. Being able to see the light in the dark is something that we find so difficult, but as with any habit, the more you do it the more naturally it comes to you. That is what self-care is. It isn't something you do once or twice and you're good; it's something that you have to work at day by day to get the strength to grow bit by bit.

I looked into where I was going, I had started to see a life without my eating disorder. It was scary to let it go but I felt like I was finally ready, so I needed to think about the future. I started Pilates classes at the local gym to start to get stronger, I took photos on my Nannys SLR and I wrote songs. I looked into photography courses, retreats, wrote a bucket list and thought about au pairing in different countries (before I remembered that kids just weren't for me). The world was open and free and I could choose whatever I wanted to do. It was so exciting. I was excited about life.

After speaking to one of the personal trainers at my gym after yet another Pilates class which had left me feeling brilliant, I looked at doing a diploma in Pilates teaching. I had been doing classes for a few months and my options were either to become a contortionist or an instructor. I figured the instructor route would probably be the best one to go down as I wasn't completely sure if the new me was claustrophobic or not and I didn't fancy squeezing myself into a suitcase or small box suspended 50 feet up in air to find out…just in case. So using the money I had saved to go to drama school, I paid for a diploma that I could start straight away.

I hadn't thought about money. I hadn't thought about talent. I hadn't thought about convenience or anything that people usually do when they go down a career path. I was purely driven by the fact that I loved it, that Pilates made me feel great and I may one day be able to share that feeling with other people. I deserved to feel good and I wanted others to feel the same.

Turns out the new me was still as spontaneous and emotionally driven as the old one!

With a new lease on life and setting off in a completely different direction that I had never fathomed before meant that I needed to really understand everything about my illness. I knew why I was ill, what made me stay ill and what I needed to do to get better, but constantly having to put myself through every day with 3 meals and 3 snacks wasn't easy. In recovery whether you are an anorexic, a bulimic or someone that suffers with an eating disorder otherwise specified (EDNOS) you at some point will have struggles with regaining weight and the restrict-binge-purge cycle.

This cycle in basic terms is a pattern in which a lot of serial dieters and people with eating disorders are stuck in, one way or another.

First there will be the restriction; starting a new diet or slimming club, skipping a meal, telling yourself you're not allowed to eat something as it makes you fat, skipping a day of food or even just the thought of not eating.

This will soon lead to our bodies getting hungry or craving the thing that we're 'not allowed'. So much so that we start to lose control over our actions as we are fueled by fear and our bodies will fight back against starvation. It only takes a few hours of us not having any food for energy and/or stressing, for our metabolism to start to slow and our bodies to start to try and work out whether it is going to have to starve and therefore keep hold of anything that it has already.

Stress eating is one of the most common forms of weight gain; our bodies create cortisol which helps to store fat and automatically thinks that what we are inhaling is what we need. This means that if we are worried about eating or going through a period of stress we cannot rule what we need to fuel our bodies and what we are taking on due to emotional eating therefore everything is kept and stored.

These cravings or lack of energy can easily lead to a 'rule break' or 'binge' which can come in all shapes and sizes; they can be as small as eating in reaction to something that we are emotionally unable to cope with, where we eat things that we have told ourselves we 'aren't allowed' and can go up to eating pretty much whatever we can find. The main things that classify a binge are the thoughts and feelings after. Often the person will feel guilty, upset or ashamed of what they have done.

They'll make up for their actions by exercising, cutting out food, restarting a diet or being sick just so that they can try to reverse what they have done and try to compensate for anything that they have eaten that they feel they shouldn't have. The guilt will usually cause the individual to promise themselves that it won't happen again; they will not touch that type of food again or allow themselves to slip off their strict 'diet' and so the restriction begins again. It is a vicious circle, one that is prevalent in our society and one that can be almost impossible to get out of.

I found it hard not to restrict, there were so many types of food that were 'bad' or 'good' and with such opinionated views on things, I stopped myself from getting better as I was constantly telling myself that if I ate a chocolate bar, I would definitely gain too much weight. My challenge from Jodie was to just keep trying. To view allowing 'bad' foods as an experiment and find out which I actually liked and which I didn't. She also stressed that I needed to stop labelling them as 'bad' and 'good' because automatically I was deciding whether I would feel guilty after eating something before it had even got close to my mouth.

I stopped trying to make up for whatever I ate. I allowed myself to sit down and accept the thoughts and feelings and made sure that I wasn't trying to compensate the food and calories by rushing around or going out for a run like I would normally do. Food was okay. It wasn't the enemy. It was energy, it was nourishment and it was going to make me better.

There was no miracle cure. There was no detox cleanse or brain rehabilitation. The answer was, in some ways, simple and although it was hard to put it into place, once I had I realised how complicated I had made my life and how much anguish and confusion I had gone through to try and be happy and healthy, when really just breaking down every part of me possible, I discovered that all that I needed to do was enjoy what I liked and take care of myself. If I was hungry I ate. I ate what I needed; never too much, never too little. I made sure I allowed myself treats every now and then so that I wasn't pushing myself into what I deemed 'healthy' and I didn't start to crave things that I 'couldn't have' because I could have whatever I wanted.

I kept a regular eating pattern that kept my metabolism and energy levels up. I found flavours and ingredients and recipes that I could experiment with. My body started to respond and work more efficiently. Although the initial weight gain ended up around my stomach and my thighs, which was hard not to worry about, after a couple of months when my body knew that I wasn't going to start starving again it distributed and I actually gained a figure and for the first time looked like a woman. Sure I had lumps and bumps in places that weren't 100% ideal in my mind but I accepted them and loved them all the same because this was all part of me. I knew that I was on the right path and I knew that in order to be able to live my life for the next 40+ years, this few months of being uncomfortable would be worth it.

I started to love my body in my own way. I saw the goodness, I saw the strength; I liked the way it moved and the way it grew stronger by the day as I started to treat it right. I had plenty of imperfections like the scars on my face and stomach, the stretch marks from gaining and losing weight so fast over the years and the muscle wastage in my hips where my body had started to practically eat itself when I was so underweight, but that was all part of me. It turned out that 'me' wasn't so bad after all. I trusted myself and found a real confidence that I hadn't known before. My body did amazing things and I truly started to appreciate it for what it was and what it could do.

This was the stepping stone that helped me to really get better as I was no longer worried all the time about what I looked like. Instead I concentrated on me, accepting who I was and the body that I had. Learning to love myself as I was in each moment and finding a lightness in who I was.

Eventually I found myself at my last appointment at the clinic, my last time at the place that I had hated so much but that had given me a new lease of life. I walked out of the double doors, ecstatic to say goodbye. I got into my Peugeot 106, pulled the driver mirror down, saw myself in the mirror, and smiled. I had done it.

Thirty

Recovery isn't a destination or a place to get to.

You don't go through the process and then you're done.

This was something that I realised in the years after finishing CBT and being discharged from the eating disorder services.

I expected recovery to just 'happen' and once it did I would feel better forever but life is never straight forward. It isn't a linear path that we tread upon. We get lost, go around in circles. We go up, down, backwards, forwards; in leaps and bounds and small steps. After leaving in 2014 I wasn't ok forever. I got lost in working for corporate companies and trying to make money, ignoring what I felt that I was called to do. On the outside life was good, but I neglected myself, my self-care and, when times got tough or relationships broke down, I would cope in the only way that I knew how and go back to the behaviours that my eating disorder appeared in.

I adapted. I told myself that it didn't really matter that I had these slip ups. It was just me; it was just how I coped but I knew deep down that if I didn't address them they would get worse. I would be ill again and unable to manage. In truth I don't think that I could really accept that it was ok not to be ok. I felt a huge responsibility to be better, I felt like I shouldn't still be having problems with eating and I felt guilt and shame that I still carried my daemons with me, even if they weren't as harmful as before.

So I didn't get help, I just continued on. I also struggled to see who I was without my eating disorder; I was in jobs that I didn't really care about. Each day I would go through the motions of life and never really love what I was doing or feel as though I was really putting into the world what I needed to. The eating disorder had defined me for so many years and if I truly got rid of it I didn't know who I was; so I controlled how I felt through food. I made sure I didn't ever overdo it but it was my coping mechanism.

Something that kept me ill was the fear of life without my illness. I had never, in all my adult life had a long period of time where I had been 'well' or totally free and to be honest part of me was scared that if I ate normally the weight would pile on like crazy and I would end up feeling awful.

When I was made to put on weight so that I got to a BMI of 20 I felt so uncomfortable in my body, I didn't feel safe and forcing that much food into my body made me want to scream. It wasn't that I felt fat but my body responded with bloating, reflux, pain and tiredness. The thought of having to feel like that to be well was counterproductive to me and something that I didn't want.

Something else that kept me stuck was my anxiety.

While I deconstructed myself in treatment and slowly started peeling away the behaviours, motives and feelings that made 'me' I uncovered it. It was like I finally got rid of one mental health illness and then God decided to give me another, just for shits and giggles.

So many days I would wake up and not be able to breathe, knowing that I would spend the next few hours breathless, heart racing, sweaty and on high alert. I would be almost paralysed with the feelings and the fear that I would have a panic attack in front of my colleagues. I would shake uncontrollably and when i'd had a period of being sick I would cramp up and lose the ability to stand or open my hands.

In some ways my anxiety felt so much worse than the eating disorder ever did, because it stopped me from participating in life and would appear in such a dramatic way that it left me feeling stupid and embarrassed. I went back on medication to try to curb it but it didn't really help. I started a course of hypnotherapy to learn how to breathe and relax which did make a difference, but wasn't the miracle answer I had been looking for.

My anxiety started to get hold of me and to control it I used food, to self-medicate, to cope, to ignore and stifle all of the rushing feelings that I had. The frustration I felt was beyond anything I had felt before: I was in the happiest place that I had ever been, my life was great. I had a well-paying job, I owned a house, I was living with the love of my life who I'd met in 2015 so why now was I struggling? Why was I pressing the self-destruct button over and again? Why was I intent on fucking things up for myself?

I had done everything that I thought I was meant to do but I was ignoring my calling and I was no longer practicing self-love and acceptance. So instead of feeling amazing when I got a better paying job, I felt nothing.

Instead of feeling like a responsible adult because I had a house, a job, a meaningful relationship, I was stressed and struggled every month. My body responded to this deep feeling of discontent and started to give me little pushes to let me know I wasn't doing what I needed to be.

But I still ignored it.

So then it started to poke.

I ignored it.

It began to shove.

I ignored it.

It slapped.

Ignored.

Stamped.

Ignored.

Kicked.

Ignored.

Shook, screamed and rugby tackled and I found
myself once again being seen by paramedics after
a spectacularly bad panic attack at my new job
that I had been at for a matter of weeks .

This attack was similar to the ones that I had before I was sent to hospital and to say that it scared me was a understatement. I had so much more to lose at this point in my life and to admit that I had relapsed meant risking everything. My sister Leila came to work to pick me up and take me to her house and in the car I admitted everything. I took the risk and said "I am not ok".

Sometimes the things that you are scared of most are the things that you need to deal with over everything else. I was so afraid that if I lost my job that I would struggle and so I clung onto something that actually made me really unhappy. I was so worried that if I finally let go of my sense of control around food that I would put on weight and never stop putting on weight. I was petrified of telling the truth in case I lost my relationship and be alone.

The reality is that fear is a calling.

My anxiety was my body trying to tell me that I needed to change. I needed to upgrade. I wasn't meant to just sit at a desk working for a big faceless corporation. I wasn't meant to obsess about food or hide my true feelings to the man that I loved. Every step I took into what I thought was the right direction was taking me further and further away from my path.

I voluntarily went back to CBT. I knew that I needed some outside help and this time I would be totally honest and engage fully. I quit my job and opened my own Pilates studio in my back garden. I taught in other studios to help me cover the bills and started to build my online Pilates and wellness business. I had no idea whether it would work or whether I would be able to cope financially but I went for it. I started listening to what it was that I needed and put my faith into the Universe believing that it would take me where I needed to go.

I followed my heart.

I finally stopped and listened to what my soul was calling me to do and embraced it.

I probably worked harder than I ever had before but this work had purpose and the long hours weren't all for someone else. I still struggled to pay the bills each month at first and never had any money but I was so much happier that it didn't matter.

I knew that all I needed to do was have faith, that if I follow what lit me up inside then the rest would eventually come together. My body and my mind responded and my anxiety sat still and said; "Finally. Thank you."

Instead of viewing the way that I coped with life by using food as something that was happening to me, I started to look at what purpose it was trying to help me with. A huge part of it was being scared to fail. I was scared that if I really honestly tried to recover and put my all into it that it wouldn't work, so I skipped the hard slog and just stayed put. But in life there is no pass or fail, we don't get to the end and get a mark on how well we did. We are here to learn and understand and grow each and every day.

Instead of focussing on the end result; being better forever, I concentrated on trying to be better just for one day. For just one day I would eat breakfast, lunch and dinner. For just one day I would listen to when my body was hungry and ask it what it wanted. For just one day I would finish eating when I was full and not worry about wasting food. For just one day I would nourish my body and move it in a way that felt good.

One day turned into two, two to three. Three to five, five to ten. Every now and then I would struggle and getting through the day would be really hard. I had days when it was just too much and the eating disorder would pull me back, but instead of letting that one moment ruin my entire week, month or year I drew a line under it and started again.

I realised that I had been waiting for the a-ha moment, the time when the world shook, colour was magnified and the stars shone brighter, to *feel* recovered when actually I had what I needed inside me all along. There was stardust in me, it was always in me and I only had to look inside to realise that I had everything that I would ever need.

There is a moment in our lives when our

mother puts us down and never picks us up again. When we go outside to play with our friends for the last time. When we are tucked in by our dad for the final night. Do you remember them?

There is no dramatic ties to these moments or deep scars that are left. We simply grow past them and move on.

Recovery is like those moments. What feels impossible and life changing is a stepping stone. My day by day approach helped me to not think too much about the bigger picture but to take each step as it came and deal with each sticking point with curiosity instead of frustration. I relaxed. I let myself be guided and I did so with love, self-love and hope. I decided to end the war with myself and instead let love in.

I paired all of the things that I learnt during my time in CBT with self-love, self-appreciation and kindness. Instead of feeling out of control and lost I felt myself slowly being guided to where I needed to be. I learnt from the mistakes that I made and the lessons from the past and stuck to truth and honesty. I was vocal about how I had felt when recovery was all about getting to a goal weight, when recovery was all about food and less about how to live. Instead of focussing on getting rid of the eating disorder I focussed on life. I followed the things that made my soul happy. I worked at something that I was passionate about. I filled my life with things that made me want to take part in each day and really be present. I finally stepped out of my comfort zone and into a place of belief and dreams and hope and love.

Everything that I had been scared of before was a moment in the past that no longer plagued me. My body responded to the nourishment I was giving it and instead of ballooning up it found its set point and didn't really budge. Without trying to control my weight my body stayed pretty much the same as it was when I started treatment, but my mind was free. I had taken all the fear, obsession and need for control, opened up my life to new possibilities and finally felt calm and at ease. Each day that went past was a step further away from my old habits and insecurities. Allowing myself grace and knowing that if I have a day where I slip up it will still be ok; it took me away from black and white thinking and allowed me to experience the world in multicolour. As a result, days turned into weeks, weeks into months and I hadn't been sick or restricted myself for the longest stretch that I ever had in ten years.

And the best part?

It hadn't felt like a massive effort.

Thirty One

2016

I am sitting on a balcony, overlooking Lake Orta in
Italy. I have dreamed of this place ever since I first
visited at 17. The cobbled streets, the peaceful quiet of
the island on the lake, the way the lights dance on the
ripples in the water.

It's my birthday. I'm officially 25 and I'm in
my favourite place in the world with the man I
love more than I ever thought I was capable of.
We'd met just over a year ago. When I finally
learnt to be ok with being on my own and stopped
looking for love- he walked into my life and
changed it forever. I'm all dressed up and ready
for dinner but first, time for being in this moment
and taking the world around me in and
appreciating being alive. The sunset, the sound of
the water and the cool breeze caressing my face.
This is bliss.

The balcony doors slide open and there he
is.

Glasses of champagne in each hand and a multipack of Haribo sweets under his arm.

'Typical' I think, 'We're going for a fancy meal in a bit and his sweet tooth is going to ruin his appetite!'

He stumbles slightly over the threshold and moves quickly to save the Haribo, letting some of the champagne spill over the edge of the glass.

'Priorities' I think as I giggle at him and his rare show of clumsiness.

We sit there in silence for a while, holding hands, listening to music and I look into his eyes. Blue like the ocean and with so much depth and subtle colours.

His eyes captivated me when we first met. It was only a year ago at a bar in Cheltenham that we met for our first date, it seems like I've known him forever. He has changed my life completely and opened me up to a new world of possibilities.

I am the happiest now that I have ever been. Not because of him, but because of who I am with him by my side; I have found my love for life again, hopes and dreams for the future and he is such a big part of that. He is the one.

My favourite song by Jasmine Thompson starts playing as we sit staring out at the beautiful vista.

"Do you know how much I love you?" he says as he looks at me bathed in the sunset.

"I think so" I say, smiling.

"I want to spend the rest of my life with you"

I smile again, the feeling is mutual. I couldn't imagine my world without him in it.

"I've got an idea" he says as he takes my hand and stands me up.

I think maybe we're going to dance and laugh a little at the idea of trying to move around the tiny balcony.

He takes the bag of Haribo and stands in front of me.

"Emily Sullivan" he says as he gets down on one knee. "Will you do me the honour of one day becoming my wife?"

I take my eyes away from his face and look into the bag, inside is a ring which he takes out and places onto my finger.

I am in disbelief, is this happening?! He's shaking, I'm shaking. We're both crying a little but with huge grins on our faces.

"Yes!"

Thirty Two

2018

My work now serves me because it serves others. It fills me up from the inside out and lights a fire in my soul. Every person that I reach inspires me to teach more. Every goal accomplished, difference they see, moment of joy that they feel, I feel too. I celebrate with them and support them whenever they need.

There is a quiet revolution happening and each person who joins unknowingly recruits more. This new movement is so powerful it changes lives. It makes you feel strong, powerful, light and free.

This revolution is shunning society's expectations of who we should be, what we should look like and instead choosing self-empowerment, self-acceptance and positivity.

Each day more men and women are
breaking from a society that promotes aesthetic
over internal.

They are throwing away the diet rule book
and uncuffing themselves from the chains of guilt
and regret.

They are listening to their bodies, nurturing
and nourishing them and moving them in a way
that makes them feel amazing.

They accept who they are in this very
moment and moving forward with positivity.

They're excusing themselves from the fight
and instead choosing a different path.

They are learning to love who they are now
in order to upgrade and live the life they want to
have in the body that they love to be in.

They no longer fear the scale or refuse to acknowledge the numbers upon it because they know now that they are not defined by them, that they are more than them. They have found freedom with knowing but not emotionally investing.

They aren't afraid to speak their truth, to admit that they struggle and know that it's ok not to be ok.

More and more men and women are finding their strength and power, stepping into the light and finding freedom.

There is a quiet revolution happening that is gaining momentum each and every day.

The world is slowly changing into a planet that loves more, gives more and appreciates more. Each person that joins adds their positive energy and receives even more in return.

You know this world. You live in it already,

you are part of this world and the people within it,
just open your heart and see it.

Thirty Three

We are made up of flesh and bone and blood.

Of muscles, of tendons and cells.

Of molecules, of atoms and nuclei...

And in every single one of those infinitesimal, teeny tiny cells there is a microscopic piece of Stardust.

On it's own it seems insignificant, powerless and weak.

But when we realise that we have the power to connect these pieces all together we find freedom and lightness.

We are all made of Stardust. The perfections and imperfections. The atoms and molecules that make up our souls and surrounding lives. Individual and identical at the same time to everyone else with their flaws and their beauty. Naturally moving and flowing freely, each individual particle colliding with the next and making up something wonderful. Something shining, something golden.

If you focus, you can feel it.

You can sense those pieces of Stardust connecting within yourself. Lighting up your fingertips, running through your veins and spreading through your hands, up your arms, into your shoulders - that golden light spreading up your neck and lighting up your face and head. Setting you free.

This feeing can run through your entire body. It vibrates and pulsates and liberates.

When you feel it, you know.

You are becoming something more than before.

Something powerful and amazing.

Beautiful and golden.

You.

You are enough.

You are more than enough.

You are the light bringer.

You are the abundant one.

You are the one with the strength and the power to be who you truly are.

Be strong.

Be happy.

Be a beacon of love, of light and of hope.

You do you.

You be you.

You love you.

You've got this.

Thank You

If you're reading this far then you have read my book from beginning to end. I have to say a huge thank you for taking the time out of your busy life to read, listen and understand my own personal journey.

It took me a good 6 years to write and edit Stardust - It began as a Wordpress blog in order to get all the thoughts and feelings out that I was going through during recovery and it soon became a platform for people to share their own experiences and connect. It was read in over 30 different countries and had over 6000 views enabling me to go to schools and universities to talk to students about mental health and eating disorders. So much happened in that time since I started writing that sometimes I felt like I wasn't sure if I would ever put it out to the world. However I've always known that I needed to share my message and my story - I've always ended up being pulled back to it. I know in my soul, that if my words are able to change the course of just one person's life, I will consider this book a success.

From my heart to yours, I hope that you have found this book of use. Whether you are someone who is struggling with your relationship with food, your body, your self worth or your mental health I hope you take my words and know that there is hope. There is always the possibility of true recovery and not just struggle. I know, I've seen it, I live it! There is life after a mental health illness and I can promise you right now that it is a good one! You just need to believe in yourself, be kind, pick yourself up when you fall and keep going, keep growing and learn to love yourself again.

If you are reading this to understand a loved one a little better, then I hope that my story has helped you to to perhaps see from a different perspective. I will never understand fully what I put my own family and friends through during my dark days. What I do know though, is that no matter how many times I pushed them away and wanted them to leave me alone they never let go. Living with a mental illness is so hard -it can also be a very self-centred disease as you kind of go inward, so as a result, it can be hard to see from an outsiders perspective. If it wasn't for the continued love and support of my family I think that my story would have ended very differently. So please, no matter how difficult it gets, remember that love is one of the most powerful forces that exists on our planet. Hold your loved one close, tell them that they are going to be ok and always protect your own happiness too.

Thank you again for taking the time to read this.

Thank you for being so uniquely you.

Thank you for being a part of the magic in this world.

Love always, Emily xx

Be Part of the Stardust

If you have enjoyed this book and would like to work with me, or find out more about me and the work that I do, look for @emjandrew on Facebook, Instagram and Twitter or head to the websites below:

www.healthybalancewithemily.com
www.emilyjandrew.com
www.instagram.com/emjandrew
www.facebook.com/healthybalancewithemily
www.pinterest.com/emjandrew
www.twitter.com/emjandrew

If you want to help to spread stardust and invite me to speak at your school/work/office/event please reach out.

If you are struggling with any type of mental health illness then this is a message for you; there are people out there who are there to help, you can find charities like Beat, Mind and more online or through your local health provider. Please reach out. Although I'm not qualified in treatment or therapy of any kind (yet) if you need someone to talk to, who will listen without judgement contact me on any of my social media channels. You are not alone.

Acknowledgments

Thank you to my wonderful family, especially Mum, Dad, my incredible step parents; Gareth and Mirela, my amazing sisters, brother and their families as well as the rest of my huge family pack for supporting me always; for never giving up, for giving me firm words when I needed to hear them, holding me tight when I needed it, keeping me grounded, laughing with (sometimes at) me and loving me no matter what.

Thank you to my beautiful best friend Kirsty whose friendship never faltered, who stuck by my side and who I've spent some of the best times in my life with - you're all I needed to keep my head above water at times (literally!). You are a ray of sunshine with so much strength - a woman of true Stardust and a friend for life.

To my wonderful close friends and hens, who brought so much joy and happiness into my life and helped me to understand that friendship isn't something that ever fades away, love never diminishes and I have so much love in my heart for you, always. You have also opened new chapters for me and I can't wait to go through life with you by my side.

A special thank you to Emily, who was so much more than a 'treatment friend'. Your strength and determination inspires me each and every day. What you are accomplishing is incredible, you're incredible and I have such a huge space in my heart that totally belongs to you.

To all the amazing staff in the NHS - please know that the work you do is so unbelievably important even if it isn't always as valued as it should be. Thank you so much for your help & support.

To Gemma & Jess who took the time to read and edit this book - giving me the confidence to finally put it out to the universe! I'm not sure I could have without you! Thank you.

To Alan, I love you to the moon and back...and back again. You have brought true love into my life and every day I feel like I love you more than the day before. Thank you for supporting me, never judging and always encouraging me to keep going, no matter what. You are one of the kindest, most loving, incredible people that I ever met and I consider myself blessed to have found you. I can't wait to continue to build our lives together and see where this crazy ride will take us. Always and forever. x

Printed in Great Britain
by Amazon

61407661R00161